Roadside History of
Yellowstone Travel

Roadside History of

Yellowstone Travel

A NATIONAL PARK GUIDEBOOK
FOR HISTORY LOVERS

Win Blevins

Mountain Press Publishing Company
Missoula, 1989

Blevins, Winfred; Blevins, Marcia Meredith

A Roadside History of Yellowstone: A National Park Guidebook for
History Lovers

1. American National Parks—Travel Guidebooks. 2. United States
Travel—Road Trips. 3.Yellowstone National Park – True Accounts. 4.
Yellowstone Park – Guide Book. 5. Yellowstone Park—History

ISBN-13: 9780692439203

DEDICATION

This book about a region of magnificent mountains, lakes, rivers, and forests is dedicated to my two long-time climbing partners, Leeds Davis and Hooman Aprin. The days I have spent in the wilds in their company are among the most pleasurable of my life.

TABLE OF CONTENTS

ABOUT THIS BOOK

History is the story of the doings of people. The scenery, geology, and the wildlife of Yellowstone National Park are wondrous. But nothing so intrigues human beings as the escapades of other human beings. And people have acted as wisely and crazily, honorably and dishonorably, bravely and timidly here as anywhere else. Perhaps more so—an extravagant setting gives birth to extravagant deeds.

In this book you will learn about Yellowstone National Park's people. The Indians who lived here (or traveled through) before the white men came. The mountain men who discovered the park for the white people, and explored it. The official government "explorers" who mapped it, and worked for Yellowstone to become the first national park. The poachers and other exploiters who threatened the park, and the men who protected it. The travelers, foreign and domestic, high-born and low-born, who sojourned here—all the travails, thrills, dramas, and serene satisfactions of the people over the park's history.

This volume is designed to be easy and enjoyable to read. You may begin at whichever of the five park entrances you use and follow the park's story as you follow the road—historic points are indicated by sights and by mileages. These points are easy to track whether you travel north to south or vice versa, clockwise or counter-clockwise on the park's main thoroughfare, the Grand Loop Road—mileages are given for both directions.

In writing this history I've had no choice but to follow the trails other writers have ridden before me—in diaries, newspaper articles, and other first-hand reports of people who were here, plus the substantial books of the corps of historians of Yellowstone. For the wider Yellowstone story I recommend that you dip into the works of these writers, particularly those who set down their own experiences. So a reading list is appended at the back of the book.

Sometimes, though, you'll find that history and legend have gotten mixed up. After a hundred years and more, it can be hard to sort one from the other. Here I've tried to label legend as legend, but to give it a place. The great tales of the park are now part of its lore, and they speak of the spirit as well as the bare fact of this fabled area.

Perhaps I've also put extra emphasis on park anecdotes that are comical—isn't that as it should be?

Winfred Blevins
Jackson Hole
March, 1989

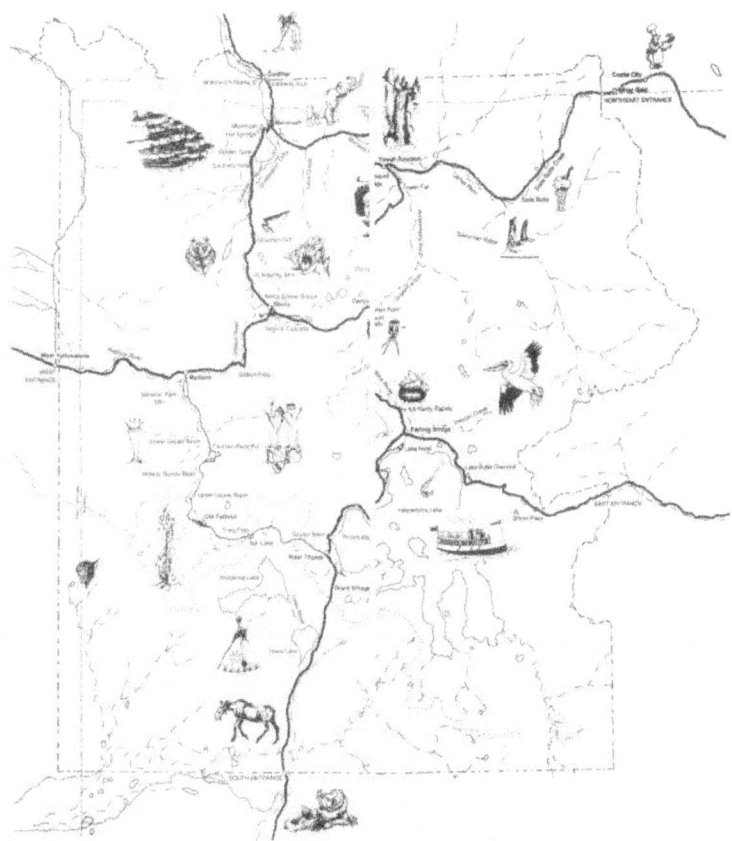

ACKNOWLEDGMENTS

My principal debt in writing this little volume has been to two National Park Service historians, the first a man I haven't met, the second a man I was lucky enough to find in the Yellowstone of today: Aubrey Haines, historian of Yellowstone Park in the 1960s, wrote the authoritative two-volume history of the park *The Yellowstone Story*, and I have kept it close at hand during the writing. Tim Manns, the current park historian, has helped me abundantly with information and counsel, and has saved me from error more than once. I am grateful to them both.

A Timeline of Yellowstone National Park

1807 or 1808: John Colter, often thought of as the first mountain man, became the first white man to see what is now the national park; he probably saw some hot springs but not geysers.

from 1825: Mountain men frequented the park, notably Jim Bridger, Osborne Russell, Joe Meek, Warren Angus Ferris, and Daniel Potts. Their tales about the thermal wonders there were mostly disbelieved.

1870: General H. D. Washburn headed an exploring expedition to the park, observing and naming important features, and perhaps giving early impetus to the idea of creating a national park.

1871: A government expedition headed by Dr. Ferdinand V. Hayden surveyed some of the park. The images created by two members of the party, painter Thomas Moran and photographer William H. Jackson, would convey the natural wonders of Yellowstone to the public powerfully.

The odometer used by the Hayden survey. These were the
first wheels ever taken into this little-known region.
—Hayden survey, W.H. Jackson photo, U.S. Geological Survey

1872: Influenced by Dr. Ferdinand V. Hayden and others of
the 1870 and 1871 surveying expeditions, Congress created
Yellowstone as the first national park.

1876: The Army's Doane Expedition set out to explore the
Snake River, and came to near-disaster.

1877: The Nez Perce Indians traversed the park during their
long, desperate, and doomed flight toward Canada; in the
park they kidnapped some tourists and had some skirmishes.

1877-82: Philetus Norris, the park's second superintendent,
pioneered park roads to principal features.

Old Faithful Geyser, ca 1878.
—Hayden survey, W.H. Jackson photo, U.S. Geological Survey

1878: The Bannock War spilled over into the park; it was the last of the Indian-Anglo armed conflicts in Yellowstone.

1883-86: Lieutenant Dan C. Kingman, the park's first road engineer, began building what became the modern Grand Loop Road.

1886: The U.S. Army took over administration of the park.

1891: Hiram M. Chittenden came to Yellowstone as a road engineer; he would become the park's first major historian, publishing in 1895 *The Yellowstone National Park.*

1891: Construction of Fort Yellowstone was started at Mammoth.

1891: Lake Hotel was begun.

1902: Yellowstone domestic buffalo herd was started.

1903: The gateway arch at the north entrance to the park was built, and dedicated by President Theodore Roosevelt.

1904: Old Faithful Inn was opened, said to be the largest log structure in the world.

1908: What may have been the biggest stagecoach robbery of the century — seventeen coaches — took place at Turtle Rock; but the amount stolen was only a little over two thousand dollars.

1915: By order of the Secretary of the Interior, automobiles were first admitted into the park on a regular basis.

1916: The National Park Service was created, and took over administration of the park from the Army.

1943: A B-17 bomber crashed in the park, killing ten of the eleven airmen aboard.

1959-70: Frank and John Craighead pioneered grizzly-bear research in the park.

1970: The last of the park's garbage dumps was closed, amid much controversy, to limit the access of bears to human food.

1981: Grant Village was completed in its present form, despite controversy over its possible impact on grizzly habitat.

1988: In an exceptionally dry summer, wildfires burned about one third of the total acreage of the park. Some fires were caused by man, some by nature. The huge conflagrations led to much public questioning of the park's natural-fire policy. Many wildlife scientists said the fires would be a powerful source for biological renewal in the park, and would benefit many animal species.

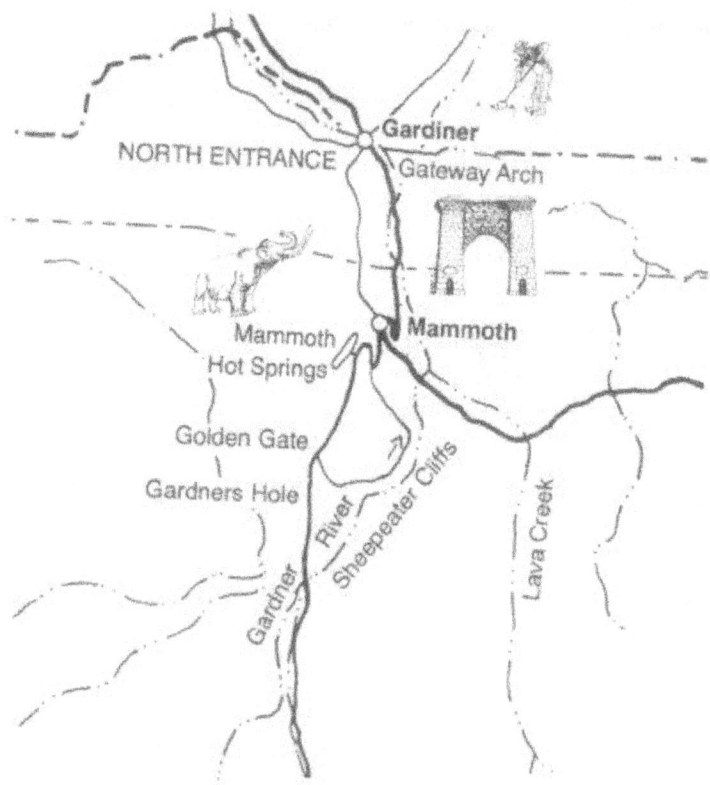

North Entrance—Mammoth Hot Springs

Chapter I

North Entrance to Mammoth Hot Springs

5 Miles

The Gateway Arch
At North Gate
Mile 6 from Mammoth Hot Springs

The huge gateway arch through which you enter the park, built in 1903, calls to mind two of the park's great supporters, Hiram M. Chittenden and President Theodore Roosevelt. Chittenden, one of the park's primary road engineers and one of its most important historians, conceived the arch, and drafted the notes from which architect Robert C. Reamer designed it. Roosevelt made a Presidential journey to the park to lay the cornerstone of the arch.

Roosevelt spoke to about 3,000 people at the dedication. Untypically for a politician, in writing about the ceremony he recorded nothing of what he said on that occasion. What he recalled instead were some wild animals he saw as he rode toward the site:

President Teddy Roosevelt officiating at the cornerstone-laying ceremonies of Roosevelt arch, Gardiner Gateway, April 25, 1903. Roosevelt said, "The scheme of Yellowstone preservation is noteworthy in its essential democracy. This park was created and is now administered for the benefit and enjoyment of the people."
—University of Montana Archives

A little over a mile from Gardiner we could see the crowd gathered around the arch waiting for me to come. We put spurs to our horses and cantered rapidly toward the appointed place, and on the way we passed within forty yards of a score of blacktails, which merely moved to one side and looked at us, and within almost as short a distance of half a dozen antelope. To any lover of nature it could not help being a delightful thing to see the wild and timid creatures of the wilderness rendered so tame; and their tameness in the immediate neighborhood of Gardiner, on the very edge of the Park, spoke volumes for the patriotic good sense of the citizens of Montana.

The inscription on the arch quotes the 1872 Act of Congress that created Yellowstone: "For the Benefit and Enjoyment of the People." Over the years this dedication has not prevented a lot of dispute about the true purposes the park. The proper domain of man and nature here is still hotly debated.

Roosevelt loved the park, and took the opportunity of dedicating the arch to spend some time in its wilds with his chum John Burroughs, the naturalist. Burroughs wrote later that "The President wanted all the freedom and solitude possible while in the Park, so all newspaper men and other strangers were excluded. Even the secret service men and his physician and private secretaries were left at Gardiner. He craved once more to be alone with nature; he was evidently hungry for the wild and the aboriginal,—a hunger that seems to come upon him him regularly at least once a year, and drives him forth on his hunting trips for big game in the West."

Roosevelt and Burroughs were lucky enough to see some bighorn sheep near Tower Fall, scurrying up and down a rock face so perpendicular that "It seemed to me impossible" to ascend and descend, Burroughs commented.

*Away from the affairs of state, President Roosevelt prepares to
ride into Yellowstone National Park.*
—University of Montana Archives

When word of the bighorns came, TR was shaving, "with coat off and a towel around his neck. One side of his face was half shaved, and the other side lathered.

'By Jove,' said the President, 'I must see that. The shaving can wait, and the sheep won't.'

"So on he came, ... coatless, hatless, but not latherless, nor towelless."

On that trip Roosevelt indulged in some rough humor. Burroughs recorded that the President sometimes got requests for help from former Rough Riders. "In camp one night TR read a letter from one who had ended up in jail in Arizona: 'Dear Colonel,—I am in trouble. I shot a lady in the eye, but I did not intend to hit the lady; I was shooting at my wife.'

"And the presidential laughter rang out over the tree-tops."

Gardner River
Mile 1 - 5 from North Gate
Mile 0 - 4 from Mammoth

The roadway here follows through the steep canyon of the Gardner River, the oldest place name in the park except for the Yellowstone River. (The Gardner River is not spelled as is the name of the town Gardiner, Montana). The river is named after the mountain man Johnson Gardner, who first trapped beaver in Gardner's Hole, a few miles south of here, in the early 1830s. An agent of John Jacob Astor's powerful American Fur Company, Johnson was according to park historian Aubrey Haines an "illiterate, often brutal trapper."

A six-horse stagecoach in Gardner Canyon. Eagle Nest rock in background.
—F.J. Haynes photo, Montana Historical Society

Minerva Terrace

Mammoth Hot Springs Area

Mammoth Hot Springs today is the park headquarters, and has been the administrative center of the park almost since its creation. In the early days the closest encroachment of civilization to the park was nearby Montana towns like Livingston and Bozeman. The line of the Northern Pacific Railroad ran up the Yellowstone Valley to these towns and brought most early visitors to the park.

In 1886 the army was ordered to take over the park's administration. Congress had failed to provide the Department of the Interior with funds to run the park, and its unique resources were suffering—vandals were chipping away at the geyser and hot-spring formations, and the game was being slaughtered wantonly. But the civilian superintendents had never had the legal authority or the enforcement personnel to protect the park. At Mammoth Hot Springs the army first built Camp Sheridan as a base for its troops, and then, beginning in 1891, Fort Yellowstone.

Fort Yellowstone
—National Park Service, Yellowstone National Park.

Much of the old fort is still visible. The large, grassy area at the center of the town is the former parade ground. The houses facing it from the south were once the officers' quarters. Behind these houses were barracks, then a row of stables, then Soap Suds Row, where the non-commissioned officers lived; it got its name from the washing and ironing the non-coms' wives did to make ends meet.

Travelers have come from all over the world to admire the remarkable terraces created by the hot springs here, and find delight in the brilliantly colored pools confined within the deposits of geyserite. Dr. Ferdinand V. Hayden, leader of a government exploring expedition to Yellowstone in 1871, recorded his impression of the hot springs enthusiastically: "The steep sides of the hill were ornamented with a series of semi-circular basins, with margins varying in height and so beautifully scalloped and adorned with a sort of bead-work that the beholder stands amazed. Add to this a snow-white ground, with every variety of shade in scarlet, green and yellow as brilliant as the brightest dyes."

But Hayden was not pleased with everything he saw, for instance, the quality of the hospitality. The "explorers" (mountain men had known the park intimately for decades) found a hotel at the hot springs, a facility variously known as the National Park Hotel, Horr and McCartney's Hotel (after the proprietors), and Mammoth Hot Springs Hotel. Hayden described this establishment's accommodations as "very primitive, consisting, in lieu of a bedstead, of 12 square feet of floor-room." Guests were obliged to provide their own blankets. The food, Hayden went on, "is simple, and remarkable for quantity rather than for quality or variety." Not every visitor, though, was unappreciative. Windham Thomas Wyndham-Quin, the Earl of Dunraven, called the Mammoth Hot Springs Hotel "the last outpost of civilization—that is, the last place where whiskey is sold."

Artist Thomas Moran standing on the Mammoth terraces—1871.
—W.H. Jackson photo, U.S. Geological Survey

James C. McCartney's cabin, erected in 1871 near Mammoth Hot Springs.
—F.J. Haynes photo, Montana Historical Society

Better accommodations were soon available, The National Hotel,
also known as the Mammoth Hot Springs Hotel, with Oscar
Swanson and his road crew on parade ground. 1883-1885.
—National Park Service, Yellowstone National Park

In 1889 a young fellow who would one day be one of the the world's pre-eminent men of letters visited the park, Rudyard Kipling. Kipling was traveling from India to England, and he was not greatly impressed by what he saw in Yellowstone. His gleeful comment about the hot-spring formations at Mammoth was that "the ground rings hollow as a kerosene-tin, and some day the Mammoth Hotel, guests and all, will sink into the caverns below and be turned into a stalactite."

Kipling's reactions to his fellow travelers were even less kind. Observing a Fourth of July celebration at the Mammoth Hot Springs Hotel, he found his British reticence offended by the American spirit of national self-congratulation:

> What amazed me was the calm with which these folks gathered together and commenced to belaud their noble selves, their country, and their "institootions" and everything else that was theirs. The language was, to these bewildered ears, wild advertisement, gas, bunkum, blow, anything you please beyond the bounds of common sense. An archangel, selling town-lots on the Glassy Sea, would have blushed to the tips of his wings to describe his property in similar terms.

In the early days of the park, Mammoth Hot Springs was the site of lots of vandalism—tourists could not be stopped from chipping off pieces of the travertine formations, or writing on them. The military, though, instituted a strict policy of disciplining offenders. One army superintendent, George Anderson, wrote that "a very picturesque figure is a sentimental youth at twilight as he transmits his name to fame by writing it upon the 'formations'—the hot spring deposits. A much more interesting figure is this same youth at sunrise the next morning, when, followed by a mounted soldier he proceeds, scrub-brush and soap in hand, to the same spot and removes the perishable evidence of his late presence."

Frederic Remington, the Western artist, voiced a malediction upon such vandals that many of us still second rousingly: "Nature has made her wildest patterns here, has brought the boiling waters from her greatest depths to the peaks which bear eternal snow, and set her masterpiece with pools like jewels. Let us respect her moods, and let the beasts she nurtures in her bosom live, and when the man from Oshkosh writes his name with a blue pencil on her sacred face, let him spend six months where the scenery is circumscribed and entirely artificial."

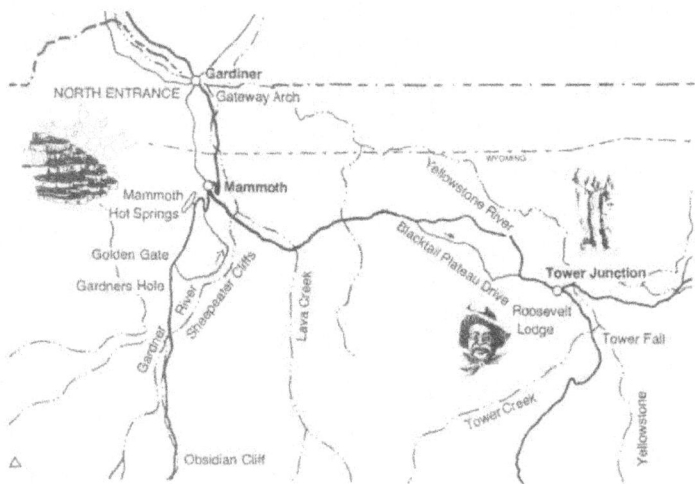

Mammoth—Tower Junction

CHAPTER II

MAMMOTH TO TOWER JUNCTION

18 Miles

Even before the park was created in 1872, a pack trail followed the approximate route of this road from Mammoth Hot Springs to Tower Junction and on to the northeast entrance of the park. Cooke City, Montana, just beyond the northeast gate, was already an active mining area.

Blacktail Plateau Drive
Mile 9.5 from Mammoth
Mile 8.5 from Tower Junction

Here a dirt road turns off to the south, Blacktail Plateau Drive. It is worth driving for several reasons of historic interest: It is the approximate route of the old Bannock Trail. The Bannock Indians, who lived on the Snake River plains of what is now Idaho, used this trail periodically in the mid-nineteenth century to cross the Rocky Mountains to the east side for buffalo hunts. Hiram Chittenden, the park's first major historian, says that through the park the trail ran "from Henry Lake across the Gallatin Range to Mammoth Hot Springs.... Thence it led across the plateau [that is, Blacktail Plateau] to the ford [of the Yellowstone River] above Tower Falls; and thence up the Lamar Valley, forking at Soda Butte, and reaching the Bighorn Valley by way of Clark's Fork and the Shoshone River."

Truman C. Everts
—National Park Service, Yellowstone National Park

Here on what was then called the Devil's Cut, Truman C. Everts was found after a grim and harrowing challenge to survival.

Everts got separated from his horse and his companions in rough country south of Yellowstone Lake in September of 1870. With his horse went his weapon, his food, and his means of making fire. Thinking that other members of his party, the exploring expedition led by General H. D. Washburn in 1870, would search diligently for him, Everts set out on what he thought was their trail. In fact, it was another direction. Ravenous, he came to a small lake filled with waterfowl, but he had no means to kill any. That night a mountain lion treed him and frightened him half out of his wits. By now the poor man was suffering terribly from the cold at night, from his hunger, and from his fears and imaginings.

Soon he discovered three life-savers: He could keep warm in the hot springs beside the lake. He could eat a certain thistle. And he could make fire with the lens of his opera glass.

After some days of rest and anxiety, during which he managed to scald his leg badly in a hot spring, Everts reached a fearful decision. He wrote later, "I knew my escape from the wilderness must be accomplished, if at all, by my own unaided exertions. This thought was terribly afflicting, and brought before me, in vivid array, all the dreadful realities of my condition. I could see no ray of hope." Thus cheerless, he set out.

Weeks passed, and he grew weaker and weaker. Once he lost his precious lens, went back after it, and luckily found it. But his days of travel were getting shorter and shorter, and his mental state was getting uncertain. He commented of himself,

> Weakened by a long fast, and the unsatisfying nature of the only food I could procure, I know that ... my mind ... was in a condition to receive impressions akin to insanity. I was constantly travelling in dreamland, and indulging in strange reveries such as I had never before known. I seemed to possess a sort of duality of being, which, while constantly reminding me of the necessities of my condition, fed my imagination with vagaries of the most extravagant character. Nevertheless I was perfectly conscious of the tendency of these morbid influences, and often tried to shake them off, but they would ever return with increased force.... Thus I lived in a world of ideal happiness, and in a world of positive suffering at the same time.

Meanwhile Everts's friends put up a reward of $600 for the recovery of his body. Collins Jack Baronett, known as Yellowstone Jack, set out with a companion to find the remains. Baronett, a Scot, had spent his life sailing the seven seas, soldiering, and looking for gold. By 1870 he knew the

Yellowstone country intimately from his prospecting in the region. He took the back trail of the Washburn party, and on Blacktail Plateau his dog started growling at something dark that Baronett took for a bear. Baronett went close to shoot the bear, and then noticed that "it was making a low groaning noise, crawling along upon its knees and elbows, and trying to drag itself up the mountain. Then it suddenly occurred to me that it was the object of my search."

Park Service historian Aubrey Haines adds that "at the time of his rescue, Everts was described as weighing about fifty pounds, his clothing was in shreds, and he had no shoes. The balls of his frostbitten feet were worn to the bone, and his scalded thigh was likewise exposed. Other areas of his body were seared and blackened, while his fingers resembled bird's claws. He was both inarticulate and irrational when found, and doubtless would soon have died of exposure to the cold sleet that was then coating the ground." He had been lost in the Yellowstone wilderness for 37 days.

Yet Jack Baronett was denied the reward. He was told that the money was offered for Everts's body only. Evidently the living man was not worth a reward.

The North Fork Fire
Miles 14 - 16 from Mammoth
Miles 2 - 4 from Tower

Here is visible a swath burned by the North Fork Fire, the largest of the historic wildfires of 1988. For a description of the major fires of that summer, and a discussion of the park's fire policies, see pp. 90-94. In late October of 1988, six weeks after this area burned, much of the ground here had been turned to ash by the intensity of the burn. It looked like a region of utter blight, a landscape of gray and black. But already, along the edge of the pavement where the little bit of rain had run off, green grass had sprung up. And some visitors found that bold bit of color a touching declaration of hope.

Pleasant Valley
Mile 17 from Mammoth
Mile 1 from Tower

Between the road and the mountains to the north lies Pleasant Valley, or Yancey's Hole, and here Uncle John Yancey built the Pleasant Valley Hotel between 1884 and 1887. It enjoyed the patronage of the novelist Owen Wister, the writer and illustrator Ernest Thompson Seton, and other notables, especially fishermen. The accommodations were basic. A guest described them like this in 1901:

Pleasant Valley Hotel, proprieter John Yancy in foreground. Photo taken by F.J. Haynes during his mid-winter expedition, January, 1887.
—Montana Historical Society

Uncle John Yancy
—National Park Service, Yellowstone National Park

An inspection of the bedrooms prove them to be large enough for a single bedstead with a box in which are washbowl, pitcher and part of a crash towel. Of the four window lights at least one was broken in every room. The cracks in the wall are pasted up with strips of newspaper.... The beds showed they were changed at least twice, once in the spring and once in the fall of the year. A little bribe on the side and a promise to keep the act of criminality a secret from Uncle John induces the maid to provide us with clean sheets."

Wister described Uncle John as a "goat-bearded, shrew-eyed, lank Uncle Sam type," and the many complaints about his rooms and food—only the whiskey seems to have passed muster—seem to have made no impression on him at all.

Tower Junction Area

The ranger's residence here is one of three remaining soldier stations in the park. The others are at Norris Junction and Bechler.

The soldier stations served to house a few soldiers at outlying locations in the park to prevent vandalism of thermal areas, enforce the campfire rules, and control the poaching, particularly of elk and buffalo. In the early decades elk, especially, were killed indiscriminately. At Mammoth Hot Springs in the spring of 1875, for instance, the Bottler brothers alone, who were local ranchers, killed 2,000 elk. A visiting party of the Secretary of War observed the slaughter in that year and asked publicly why the park superintendent allowed it. But the poor superintendent had neither the laws nor the manpower to stop the poachers.

The Soldier Station at Thumb
—F.J. Haynes photo, Montana Historical Society

After 1886, when the army took over the park's administration, soldiers were posted to outlying stations to slow the poachers down. These postings meant lonely billets for months in remote locations such as Soda Butte, Riverside, Norris, Lower Geyser Basin, and Shoshone Station. In the winter months the only communication with other human being was via "snowshoe" parties. These "Norwegian snowshoes" were what we would call cross-country skis, very long skis, used with a single long pole. Many of the soldiers, and later the scouts and rangers, became expert at travel on these skis and in techniques of winter survival. When carrying loads uphill, they kept the skis from sliding backwards downhill by attaching elk hide to the bottoms, with the hair pointing backward. And they went downhill rapidly enough.

Lispenard Stewart party with the results of a hunting trip,
1887 near Mammoth Hot Springs.
—F.J. Haynes Photo, Montana Historical Society

This patroling on skis was rough and serious business. Frederic Remington, the Western illustrator, describes the soldiers' patrols of the 1890s:

> The rounds of the Park are ... made by mounting the cavalry on the ski, or Norwegian snowshoe, and with its aid men travel the desolate snow-clad wilderness from one "shack" to another. Small squads or three or four men are quartered in these remote recesses of the savage mountains, and remain for eight months on a stretch. The camps are provisioned for arctic siege, and what is stranger yet is that soldiers rather like it, and freely apply for this detached service.

About the same time the novelist and journalist Emerson Hough, (author of *The Covered Wagon*, among other tales) took a fling at skiing on these contraptions, and left us a vivid description of his experience:

> Billy [Billy Hofer, a veteran park packer and hunting guide] took me out where the snow was about 11 ft. deep and introduced me to a pair of long, low, rakish, piratical-looking things, with a good deal of overhang forward, and — as I learned later — without any center-board, keel or moral principles anywhere in their composition .... A pair of skis make about the liveliest way of locomotion, if you give them a chance, of anything on earth, and if you don't think they are alive and full of soul, you just try them and see. They've got a howling, malignant devil in every inch of their slippery surface, and the combination will give the most blase and motionless man on earth a thrill a minute for a good many minutes.

Skiing Party near Obsidian Cliff, Haynes mid-winter expedition, 1887.
—F.J. Haynes photo, Montana Historical Society

The purpose of the ski patrols, though, was serious—to stop the killing of the herds of elk, buffalo, deer, antelope, and bighorn sheep that were among the park's prime attractions. Soon the poaching was mostly under control, perhaps because the people of the towns near the park realized the truth of Teddy Roosevelt's comment: "A deer wild in the woods is worth to the people of the neighborhood many times the value of its carcass, because of the way it attracts sportsmen, who give employment and leave money behind them."

The park superintendents then turned their attention to another problem, the control of predators, primarily coyotes, wolves, wildcats, grizzlies, and mountain lions, which they saw as destructive of the prized game herds.

They quickly created an unanticipated problem: With predators diminishing, the numbers of elk could increase drastically. That started a heated debate about the complicated relationship of predators and game animals that persists to this day—observe the current controversy about re-introducing the wolf into the park, and add to it the long-standing arguments about the size of the elk herds, which are seen by different groups as both too small and too large.

Back there in the 1890s, in the words of Park Service historian Aubrey Haines, the military administration formulated some new policies: "The fauna of the park was to be protected absolutely, not even excepting those animals of 'fang and claw' ... ; the forests were to be protected absolutely, even if the soldiers had to be metamorphosed into fire fighters to do it, and the thermal features were to be protected absolutely, though it meant a constant struggle with name scribblers, pebble tossers, and souvenir pickers."

Unfortunately, the neighboring ranchers did not agree that predators should be left uncontrolled—these predators were (the ranchers claimed) feeding on their cattle and sheep. And there we go again, back into the never-ending quarrel.

First automobile through park at Old Faithful Inn. August 1, 1915
—F.J. Haynes photo, Montana Historical Society

Roosevelt Lodge, named for Teddy Roosevelt, a tent camp in the early days, became an auto camp in 1920s and thus a symbol of a revolution in the way people came to the park and enjoyed it. In the early years of this century automobiles were forbidden in the park because they were likely to scare the horses of carriages and wagons and endanger drivers and passengers. The car was first admitted officially by order of the Secretary of the Interior in 1915. Admission for single-seaters was $5, 5-seaters, $7.50, and 7-seaters, $10.00—prices comparable to today's, but in more valuable dollars. The speed limit was 20 miles an hour generally, 12 when going up, 10 when coming down, and 8 when approaching sharp curves. You were clocked from one soldier station to the next, and if you arrived too soon, you got a ticket for speeding.

Within a decade the park was full of auto campgrounds, patronized enthusiastically by an eager public. Thus did technology entirely overturn the old way of doing things.

In its first several decades park visitors were either exemplars of the carriage trade, sagebrushers, or practitioners of the Wylie Way. The carriage-trade style came first in chronology and in the hearts and minds of the park's concessionaires, but not necessarily of the public. From the first the owners of the railroads envisioned Yellowstone as a hugely successful commercial resort. They pictured thousands of visitors traveling west by rail each year, touring the park in big Concord coaches drawn by as many as six horses and carrying up to 29 passengers, and living in style at sumptuous hotels—all these facilities, naturally, to be owned by the railroads or firms they controlled. Affluence was to be the entrance requirement to the park. And this carriage trade did develop, though it never proved profitable.

"Like it was — I'm up with the driver."
—Montana Historical Society

Car camping in Yellowstone National Park
—National Park Service, Yellowstone National Park.

From the first the "sagebrushers" also came—people who toured by foot, horseback, or even bicycle, cooked out, and slept on the ground. Since they meant little to the concessionaires, or to the tip-hungry hotel staffs, they met a certain amount of resentment. Presumably, they didn't care.

Around the turn of the century William W. Wylie, a school superintendent from Bozeman, Montana, hit on a middle way between the carriage trade and sagebrushing—permanent tent camps. The Wylie Way quickly proved popular. It was economical and pleasantly informal. Wylie's young and cheerful staff pleased the guests with sound interpretive information, and provided impromptu entertainment in the evenings.

Wylie's tents did get crowded. One guest remarked that "during the height of the season the principle upon which the beds are populated is said to be the addition of visitors so long as they may arrive, or until the occupants 'go for their guns.'" Though opposed by railroad interests, camping in permanent tents survived to the end of the stagecoach era.

Wylie's Camp Roosevelt, 1915
—Haynes Studio, Montana Historical Society

The Shaw and Powell tourist tent camp near Tower Fall
—F.J. Haynes photo, Montana Historical Society

The automobile, though, turned the traditional ways of visiting the park on their heads. After World War II even the railroads bent their knees to the car—they began closing their spur lines to the towns near the park.

Today automobiles completely dominate park transportation, and for what both the National Park Service and the public judge to be good reason. Cars have made visits to the park inexpensive, and thus available to everyone, which seems to most people democratic. Some people do complain about the noise, pollution, and crowding that the automobile brings. But very few think that this dire prediction by Lord James Bryce in 1912 has come true: "If Adam had known what harm the serpent was going to work, he would have tried to prevent him from finding lodgment in Eden; and if you were to realize what the result of the automobile will be ... you will keep it out."

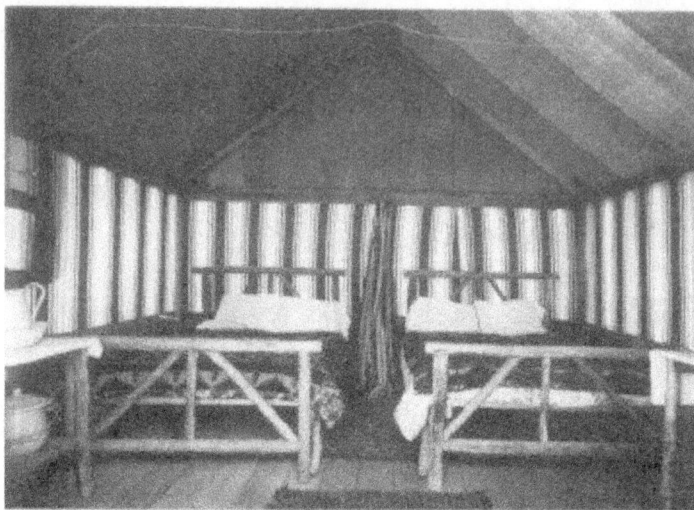

Interior view of Shaw and Powell tent camp
—Montana Historical Society

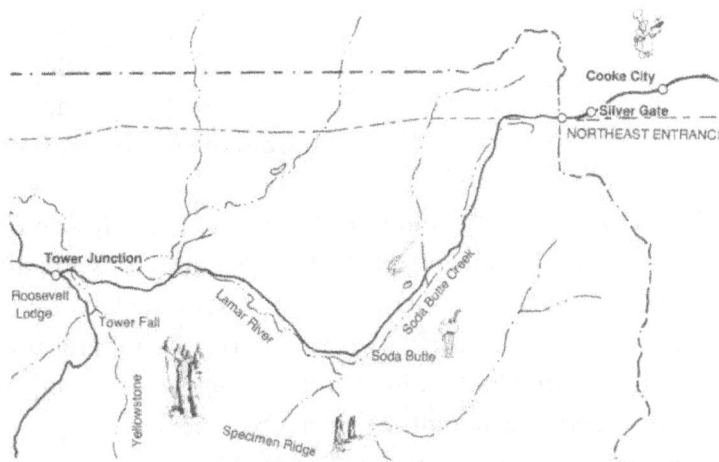

Tower Junction—Northeast Entrance

Chapter III
Tower Junction to
Northeast Entrance

29 Miles

Baronett's Bridge
Mile 1 from Tower Junction
Mile 28 from the Northeast Gate

Downstream of the modern bridge over the Yellowstone River is the site of the first bridge over this mighty stream. Baronett's Bridge was built by Collins Jack Baronett in 1871, before the park existed, to serve the mining traffic to and from Cooke City, Montana. Yellowstone Jack, as he was called, was one of the great characters of the park's early history. A Scot, Baronett went to China as a sailor, to California as a gold-seeker, to the arctic as a whaler, and to Australia and Africa, again looking for gold. From the 1860s to the turn of the century, Baronett scouted and prospected in the Yellowstone region.

Baronett's Bridge on the Yellowstone River was built in 1871, and was partially destroyed by the Nez Perce Indians in 1877. It was rebuilt later by Jack Baronett.
—F.J. Haynes photo, 1882, Montana Historical Society.

Valley of the Lamar River
Miles 8-13 from Tower Junction
Miles 16-21 from the Northeast Gate

This valley of the Lamar River was frequented by mountain men and Indians before Yellowstone Park was even dreamt of. It is a natural and easy route from the tangle of mountains of the Yellowstone Plateau to the Clarks Fork (of the Yellowstone) and so to the buffalo plains beyond.

The trapper Osborne Russell wandered into this valley, which he called Secluded Valley, in the 1830s and, struck by its beauty, spoke for many observers since: "I almost wished

I could spend the remainder of my days in a place like this where happiness and contentment seemed to reign in wild romantic splendor."

Lamar Station
Mile 10 from Tower Junction
Mile 19 from the Northeast Gate

Here at Lamar Station the Lamar Buffalo Ranch actually raised buffalo from 1907 to the 1960s, the semi-domesticated herd interbreeding with the wild herd. After that time, in accordance with new Park Service thought, the buffalo were no longer fed but were allowed to thrive, or not, in a natural "vignette of primitive America."

Buffalo herd near Mammoth
—J.E. Haynes photo, 1910, Montana Historical Society

The domestic herd was started at Mammoth Hot Springs between 1902 and 1905 by Charles J. Jones, known as Buffalo Jones, a game warden who had been a buffalo breeder in

Kansas. Jones brought buffalo cows from Montana and bulls from Texas to get the new herd started. He was an old-hand frontiersman, and apparently daring: He once caught a mountain lion in a mine shaft and brought it back tied behind his saddle. Teddy Roosevelt reports that Jones used to rope bears that had been feeding in garbage dumps to take tin cans off their paws. But he could not get along with the other park employees. A teetotaller himself, he challenged the dependability and honesty of men who drank, smoked, or played poker, and ended up by so alienating everyone that they would not speak to him. He was obliged to resign.

Specimen Ridge
Mile 12 from Tower Junction
Mile 17 from the Northeast Gate

A geology exhibit sign here points out Specimen Ridge, running about parallel to the road on the southeast side. The ridge is a layer cake of fossil forests, and may be the source of one of the great park yarns, mountain man Jim Bridger's tale of petrified light. As historian Hiram Chittenden repeats the story,

> There exists in the Park country a mountain which was once cursed by a great medicine man of the Crow nation. Everything upon the mountain at the time of this

dire event became instantly petrified and has remained so ever since. All forms of life are standing about in stone where they were suddenly caught by the petrifying influences, even as the inhabitants of ancient Pompeii were surprised by the ashes of Vesuvius. Sage brush, grass, prairie fowl, antelope, elk, and bears may there be seen as perfect as in actual life. Dashing torrents and the spray mist from them stand forth in arrested motion as if carved from rock by a sculptor's chisel. Even flowers are blooming in colors of crystal, and birds soar with wings spread in motionless flight, while the air floats with music and perfumes siliceous, and the sun and the moon shine with petrified light!

Harry Yount
—W.H. Jackson photo, 1874, U.S. Geological Survey

Yount's Cabin
Mile 13 from Tower Junction
Mile 16 from the Northeast Gate

Here near the confluence of Soda Butte Creek and the Lamar River, between the creek and the river, in the 1880s was Yount's Cabin. Harry Yount, known as Rocky Mountain Harry, was an old-hand frontiersman and briefly a gamekeeper in the park. Yount's Peak, the source of the Yellowstone River southeast of the park, is named for him.

Soda Butte and Soldier Station
Mile 15 from Tower Junction
Mile 14 from the Northeast Gate

Opposite Soda Butte, the conspicuous travertine mound on the southeast side of the road, in the early decades was a soldier station, a post housing the soldiers whose duty was to guard the park's wild game against poachers.

Entrance Station
Mile 29 from Tower, at the Northeast Gate

The entrance station here is listed as a National Historic Landmark as an example of Rustic Architecture.

Tower Junction — Grand Canyon

Chapter IV
Tower Junction to Grand Canyon

17 Miles

Tower Fall
Mile 2 from Tower Junction
Mile 15 from Canyon

Tower Fall, which is depicted on the cover of this book in a lovely watercolor by Thomas Moran, seems fairy-like in a country of grander waterfalls. Lieutenant Gustavus Doane, one of the leaders of the Washburn exploratory expedition in 1870, left us an early description that many people will agree with even today: "Nothing can be more chastely beautiful than this lovely cascade, hidden away in the dim light of overshadowing rocks and woods, its very voice hushed to a low murmur."

The fall is named after the conspicuous row of black basalt gendarmes. At its lip was once precariously perched a large rock—the members of the Hayden expedition jokingly bet on how soon it would fall. The rock fell 115 years later, in 1986.

Tower Fall
—W.H. Jackson photo, 1871, U.S. Geological Survey

The half-mile trail down from the view point offers not only a splendid view of the fall from the bottom, but another up the Yellowstone River to Bannock Ford. This is where the Bannock Indians crossed the river on their periodic trips to the buffalo plains. The Yellowstone offers few places shallow enough for a safe ford.

John Colter, the first white man to see Yellowstone, probably also crossed the river here. A member of the Lewis and Clark expedition, Colter decided to stay in the mountains when the captains took their expedition home. Probably he was enamored of the high lonesome. Sent out by the fur trader Manuel Lisa to contact Indians in 1807, Colter turned his journey into a huge ramble—from the mouth of the Big Horn River on the Yellowstone River clear to Jackson Hole, then north into what is now Yellowstone National Park, and back to the fort, over 500 miles of wandering.

Colter's route through Yellowstone Park is unknown, but most scholars think that he crossed the Yellowstone River here at Bannock Ford and followed the Lamar River and Soda Butte Creek east to Clarks Fork.

It was on this trip that Colter saw boiling springs—not in Yellowstone Park but at the forks of the Shoshone River near Cody, Wyoming; when he told his tale to other mountain men and around St. Louis, he got an undeserved reputation as a liar.

The gallant young trapper Joe Meek got lost alone in Yellowstone when he was a mere pilgrim, and came upon some of the thermal features. His description of them is vivid and exaggerated enough to qualify him as a champeen yarner among the mountain men.

Joe Meek

No skill defined the mountain man better than his ability to tell tall tales. An old-hand scout, once a trapper, might string along some emigrants with a persuasive yarn about a hand-to-hand fight he had with a grizzly bear, for instance, and cap it straight-faced with the information that in the end he was killed and et by the bear.

Jim Bridger, in particular, got himself a bad reputation for these stories among people who didn't catch on. And sometimes listeners couldn't tell what was the literal truth and what was a stretcher. The editor of a Western newspaper got a full account of the wonders of Yellowstone from Bridger in the 1840s. But the editor didn't print this big scoop because he feared he'd be "laughed out of town if he printed any of 'old Jim Bridger's lies.'" The historian Hiram Chittenden calls Bridger "the greatest romancer of the West of his time," the creator of so many exaggerations that "the truths that he told about Yellowstone were classed with the fairy tales he told of the same region, and both were set down as the harmless vaporings of a mind to which truth had long been a stranger."

The many trappers who followed Colter to Yellowstone in the 1820s and 1830s to hunt beaver left various important place names: Colter Peak was named for Colter long after his death. Gardner's Hole and the Gardner River were called from the early days for the American Fur Company man Johnson Gardner. Bridger Lake, honoring Bridger, is just outside the park, as is Henry Lake, named for the fur trader Andrew Henry. The park's principal mountains, along the east side, were called by the trappers the Yellowstone Mountains, but this name was subsequently changed to the Absaroka Mountains, the word for the Crow tribe in their own language. Other names left by the mountain men are Burnt Hole, Firehole River, Elephant Back, Alum Creek, and Sulphur Mountain.

The Chittenden Road
Mile 8.5 from Tower Junction
Mile 8.5 from Canyon

The Chittenden Road, named for the park road engineer and historian Hiram M. Chittenden, leaves the highway here toward the summit of Mount Washburn. General H. D. Washburn, head of the important Yellowstone exploring expedition of 1870, rode to this summit to get a panoramic view of the country. A year later Dr. Ferdinand Hayden, head of that year's U. S. Geological Survey of Yellowstone, took in the same view and described it:

> The view from the summit is one of the finest I have ever seen ... an area of fifty to a hundred mile radius in every direction could be seen more or less distinctly. We had a first glimpse of [Yellowstone Lake]. To the south are the Tetons, monarchs of all they survey, their summits covered with perpetual snow. Southwest, an immense area of dense pine forests extends for one hundred miles. To the north we get a full view of the valley of the Yellowstone, with the lofty ranges that wall it in.

Thomas Ewing, who toured the park with his father, General William T. Sherman, had a different sentiment when he saw the view from Mount Washburn: "Society in general goes to the mountains not to fast but to feast and leaves their glaciers covered with chicken bones and egg-shells." Lovers of untrammeled nature will be distressed to learn that the date of Ewing's comment was 1877, just five years after the creation of the park.

Dunraven Pass
Mile 13 from Tower Junction
Mile 4 from Canyon

Dunraven Pass and nearby Dunraven Peak are named for Windham Thomas Wyndham-Quin, the Earl of Dunraven, who visited the park in 1874 and in 1876 published a book about his experiences here, *The Great Divide.*

Photo outfit at the summit of Mt. Washburn
—W.H. Jackson photo, U.S. Geological Society

Hiram Chittenden about 1904
—National Park Service, Yellowstone National Park

The Area of the Grand Canyon
of the Yellowstone River

The walls of this immense canyon, the two huge waterfalls, and the river below have drawn people to see them like few sights in the world. It may be, as many people think (including the historian Hiram Chittenden), that the ochre walls of this canyon gave the Yellowstone River its name, which the French took from one of the Indian names for the river. But it is more likely that the Indian name comes from the canyon rimrock much further downstream — it is also yellow.

To get good views of the canyon and the Upper Falls and Lower Falls of the Yellowstone, you must take at least two short drives: First go east from Canyon Junction along the north rim of the canyon to Inspiration Point, Grandview Point, and Lookout Point. This road leads back to the Grand Loop Road after less than two miles. Then, 2.5 miles south of the Junction, take the drive along the south rim to Artist Point for a spectacular view of the Lower Falls.

Artist Point got its name from the painter Thomas Moran, who toured the park with the surveying expedition led by Dr. Ferdinand V. Hayden in 1871. Moran was at this time little known, but later became celebrated for his paintings of the national parks, and was long regarded as the dean of American landscape painters. On seeing the Grand Canyon of the Yellowstone, according to Hayden, Moran "exclaimed with a kind of regretful enthusiasm that these tints were beyond the resources of human art." Nevertheless, from this spot Moran did a watercolor sketch of the canyon, and from that sketch rendered the famous oil painting *The Grand Canyon of the Yellowstone*, which now hangs in the Smithsonian Museum in Washington, D.C. Many of the paintings Moran did on this trip were reproduced in

43

Hayden's book *Yellowstone National Park and the mountain regions of portions of Idaho, Nevada, Colorado and Utah,* published in 1876.

The Lower Falls of the Yellowstone River
—W.H. Jackson photo, 1871, U.S. Geological Survey

The pioneer Western photographer William Henry Jackson was also along on the Hayden expedition. His photographs have now become synonymous with certain scenes in Yellowstone in the public mind. Hayden gave Jackson prints to members of Congress to influence the legislators to vote in favor of creating the first national park the next year.

The early explorers tried to capture something of the canyon in words as well as paint. A member of the Folsom expedition in 1869, after nearly walking his horse into the canyon near Artist Point when not looking, "discovered" the canyon. Expedition leader David Folsom later wrote that "language is inadequate to convey a just conception of the awful grandeur and sublimity of this masterpiece of nature's handiwork." Nevertheless, other wordsmiths tried to find adequate language. Perhaps one of the best efforts come from W. O. Owen, who reached the canyon as a participant in the first bicycle tour of the park in 1883 (if you can imagine bicycles in the park in 1883). Wrote Owen,

We reached Lookout Point and turned our eyes westward on the grandest canon of all those that pierce the Rocky Mountains. The awful heights and yawning depths bewildered us. All around are castellated peaks, thousands of pinnacles and endless rocky spires rearing their craggy heads aloft in infinity of form, height and opulence of color. The graceful front of rocky walls stands out sharp and terrible, sweeping down in broken crag and cliff to the mighty river, which distance reduces to a foamy ribbon, upon the lip of which the depth has laid its silent finger. But the picture is not yet complete. Over the whole is thrown a rich mantle of golden tint, enveloping crag and cliff in a dreamy cloud of color, and softening the Gothic outline of giant spires, which stand like sentinels, on the brink of the gorge.

The canyon, though, has not been admired so universally that it prohibits attempts at exploitation. The Western novelist Owen Wister loved the park and traveled through it extensively on horseback. He recounts one group's idea of exploiting the Lower Falls:

> Boutelle [Captain Frazier A. Boutelle, an acting park superintendent] had a hard time to stop a commercial clique from installing an elevator at the Lower Falls. Politics was behind it, as usual. To put a lot of machinery by those Falls at the head of the canon, where the sublime merges with the exquisite, and which alone is worth crossing the continent to see, would have been an outrage more abominable than the dam at Jackson Lake.

Owen Wister on horseback at Mammoth Hot Springs, 1891.
—F.J. Haynes photo, Montana Historical Society

"But why should your refined taste," objected a lover of the multitude to whom I told this, "interfere with the enjoyment of the plain people?"

"Have the plain people told you or anybody that the one thing they lie sleepless craving for is an elevator to go up and down by those falls the way they do in hotels?"

"They would like it if it was there."

"Of course they would. Is that a reason to vulgarize a supreme piece of wild natural beauty for all time? How are the plain people to learn better things than they know if you lower to their level everything above it?"

But who could convince a female philanthropist?

Such remarks must have caused, half a century ago when Wister wrote them, a controversy about elitism. They would cause the same controversy today, and another about sexism.

Grand Canyon of the Yellowstone from the east bank
—W.H. Jackson photo, 1871, U.S. Geological Survey

Chapter V

Canyon to Fishing Bridge

16 miles

Hayden Valley
Miles 6 - 8 from Canyon
Miles 8 - 10 from Fishing Bridge

The broad, open land stretching west toward Yellowstone's central plateau is the Hayden Valley, one of the most common places in the park to see buffalo. It is named for Dr. Ferdinand V. Hayden, head of a Yellowstone expedition for the U.S. Geological Survey in 1871. Hayden, an enthusiastic geologist trained as a medical doctor, recognized that this valley was once the bed of a great lake, of which Yellowstone Lake is a only a remnant. In addition to the technical services of the survey, Hayden brought along two artists of stature, painter Thomas Moran and photographer W. H. Jackson, who did a great deal to show the wonders of Yellowstone to the public at large.

Dr. F. V. Hayden (seated) and Walter Paris
—U.S. Geological Survey

Canyon — Fishing Bridge

Hayden Valley was also a principal site of the grizzly bear research done in Yellowstone by two brothers who are also scientists, John and Frank Craighead, from 1959-1970. Their Yellowstone field work was the first intensive study of the grizzly; in it they pioneered techniques of tracking animals with radio collars later commonly used by researchers and game managers world-wide. From that field work the Craigheads produced a number of scientific papers, and Frank Craighead wrote a popular book, *The Track of the Grizzly*, which gave early warning of that creature's deteriorating status in Yellowstone.

The Craigheads' bear research in Yellowstone ended in 1970 when they and the park administration grew unhappy with each other. The Park Service thought that the Craigheads, instead of simply doing research, were trying to influence bear policy, which should not have been their role, in the administration's view. Frank Craighead says they were doing no such thing. He believes that the superintendent did not like having researchers in the park who were not under his control. He says that the park "insisted on censoring our news releases, talks, popular articles, and technical articles. As scientists, we couldn't permit that."

Frank, left, and John Craighead holding receiver for tracking bears
at Dunraven Pass in Yellowstone Park, 1967.
—Courtesy John and Frank Craighead

Alum Creek
Mile 5 from Canyon
Mile 11 from Fishing Bridge

Alum Creek is said to have gotten its name from Old Gabe, the Blanket Chief, Jim Bridger himself. It seems that one day Jim rode up the creek several miles and then back. He noticed on the way back that he didn't have to go as far as on the way up. "Seeking the cause," says historian Hiram Chittenden, "he found it to be the astringent quality of the water, which was saturated with alum to such an extent that it had the power to pucker distance itself."

Later stage drivers would tell about fording the creek with their big coaches, only to find on the other side that their outfits had shrunk to Shetland ponies and a buggy.

The Mud Volcano
Mile 10 from Canyon
Mile 6 from Fishing Bridge

The Mud Volcano was named (though probably not discovered) by the Washburn exploring expedition in 1870. The journalist Charles Dudley Warner visited the Mud Volcano in 1896 and later recorded his impressions in a piece in *Harper's New Monthly Magazine:*

> The mud-geyser ... is, I suppose, the most disgusting object in nature.... On the side of a hill, at the bottom of a deep sloping pit, is a sort of cave, like the lair of a wild beast, which perpetually vomits a compound of mud, putty, nastiness. Over the mouth seems to be a concave rock, which prevents the creature from spouting his filth straight up like a geyser. Against this obstacle, with

a thud, every moment the vile fluid is flung, as if the beast were in a rage, and growling because he could not get out, and then through the orifice the mud is flung in spiteful spits and gushes of nastiness. And the most disgusting part of it is that this awful mixture cannot get out, and the creature has to swallow it again, and is perpetually sick to nausea. It is the most fascinatingly loathsome thing in the world.

**Buffalo Ford
Mile 11 from Canyon
Mile 5 from Fishing Bridge**

Buffalo Ford (it's officially known as Nez Perce Ford but popularly called Buffalo Ford) is where the Nez Perce Indians crossed the Yellowstone River on the their flight from the U. S. Army toward Canada in 1877. Their rebellion, which many modern Americans see as heroic, lasted for three months and 22 days; they covered more than 1500 miles in their flight, and fought at least fifteen engagements. Their bid for freedom ended in the Bear Paw Mountains just 30 miles from the Canadian border. (For more about their experiences in Yellowstone, see the entry under Nez Perce Creek on pp. 76-79.

Buffalo Ford is also one of the most popular fly-fishing spots in the park. Now the fish caught are native Yellowstone cutthroats, but fish stocking had a long history in the park.

As early as 1889 whitefish and several varieties of trout were stocked in Glen Creek, Gibbon River, Firehole River, Twin Lakes, Lava Creek, and the Yellowstone River above the falls. Non-native fish were thus introduced to park streams, and incompatible species were accidentally put together. Early scientists thought they could keep the incompatible fish in different watersheds, but one researcher proved that fish can cross from watershed to watershed even over the continental divide. That led him to exclaim, "Bridger is vindicated." One yarn attributed to Jim Bridger concerned a place where fish could cross from the Atlantic to the Pacific and back again. Isa Lake, in Craig Pass, would be one such place if it had any fish. Two Ocean Pass, south of the park, is another such place, and has the fish traffic.

Though stocking fish in the park ended in 1958, descendants of stocked fish still populate Yellowstone's waters.

Le Hardy Rapids
Mile 13 from Canyon
Mile 3 from Fishing Bridge

LeHardy Rapids got its name from a minor disaster on what was probably the first boat trip on the Yellowstone River by white people. Paul LeHardy was a topographer with the Corps of Engineers reconnaissance expedition led in the park in 1873 by Captain William A. Jones. At the outlet of the Yellowstone River, LeHardy and another man decided to go by raft instead of horseback for a while. After a pleasant three miles, they came to these rapids and soon realized that it was "now too late for anything except to trust to luck." They ran their raft onto a rock, where the back end got sucked to the shallow bottom. They threw their gear to shore, breaking LeHardy's French shotgun, and hoofed it toward Canyon.

Regulations now forbid boating on the Yellowstone River in the park, in order to preserve it as a refuge for aquatic wildlife. Some daredevils brave the lower sections, and whopping fines, anyway.

The Fishing Bridge Area

The commercial facilities in the Fishing Bridge area are now a focus of heated controversy. Some human beings want this spot for a store, service station, museum, campground, recreational vehicle park, and the like—but grizzly bears want it for eating, sleeping, and raising cubs. The consequence has been what is politely known as human-bear conflict. On occasion the results have been not only impolite but bloody.

Environmentalists have been crusading for the elimination of most commercial developments at Fishing Bridge to save the threatened grizzly. Commercial interests, particularly those from the nearest town, Cody, Wyoming, have fought to retain the developments. Grant Village was built in the late 1970s and early 1980s partly to allow the closing of the facilities at Fishing Bridge, but so far political pressures have kept most of the facilities open. The park administration's most recent proposal is to reduce the number of people in the area by closing the Park Service campground. The final decision will be made in the courts or via political compromise.

The Fishing Bridge Museum has been named a National Historic Landmark as an example of Rustic Architecture.

"Hold-up" bears in Yellowstone in 1923.
—W.T. Lee photo, U.S. Geological Survey

Fishing Bridge—East Entrance

Chapter VI
Fishing Bridge to East Entrance

27 miles

Pelican Creek
Mile 1.5 from Fishing Bridge
Mile 25.5 from the East Entrance

Pelican Creek was the site of some trappers' camp in the summer of 1839, among them Osborne Russell. Blackfeet Indians attacked the camp and stole the trappers' "possibles" (as they called their gear) and horses. Russell and company had to walk out for help—they walked clear to Fort Hall in what would later be Idaho. Just another hazard in the life of the mountain man.

Pelican Creek is now "the best grizzly habitat in the park," according to one park official, a likely spot to see bears—and unfortunately to get into trouble with them.

Advancing civilization doesn't make the the big silvertip any less dangerous. In the summer of 1984 a Swiss woman was killed by a grizzly north of Pelican Valley. In October of 1986 a Montana man photographing a griz was attacked and killed near Otter Creek after approaching a grizzly bear too closely. Bear researchers say that human deaths, and bear deaths, are unavoidable as long as the two species use the same areas too intensively. The bear deaths follow the human deaths because the Park Service kills bears which are regarded as trouble-makers. And the Yellowstone bear population is already threatened. The solution, according to the Park Service and most biologists, is to keep people away from the bears' living quarters, and to keep bears from getting people's food.

Lake Butte Overlook
Mile 9.5 from Fishing Bridge
Mile 17.5 from the East Entrance

Here a side road goes toward Lake Butte Overlook, which affords a fine panoramic view of the lake and its islands. One of the early appreciations we have of the lake is from the 1869 park explorer David Folsom, who found himself entranced by "this inland sea, its crystal waves dancing and sparkling in the sunlight as if laughing with joy for their wild freedom. It is a scene of transcendent beauty which has been viewed by few white men, and we felt glad to have looked upon it before its primeval solitude should be broken by the crowds of pleasure seekers which at no distant day will throng its shores."

Two years later some men of the Hayden surveying expedition ventured forth onto the lake from the north (right-hand) shore in a twelve-foot sailboat named the *Annie.* They'd brought pieces for the framework, and covered them with canvas. In this boat James Stevenson and a companion sailed to the timbered island near the north shore, which Dr. Ferdinand Hayden named Stevenson Island for his able assistant.

Annie, *the first boat on Yellowstone Lake, 1871.*
—W.H. Jackson photo, National Park Service, Yellowstone National Park.

A Bear Incident
Mile 14 from Fishing Bridge
Mile 13 from the east entrance

About here in 1916 some men hauling hay up Sylvan Pass were attacked by a grizzly, and one teamster was killed. The next day a terrier wandered into their camp, evidently lost. But the foreman, who didn't like dogs, left the critter out in the cold. That night Old Ephraim, the griz, came back. This time the terrier raised a ruckus and the crew drove the bear off, the dog nipping at its heels all the way. The crew then got ready for Old Ephraim—they baited a barrel with garbage and charged the opening with dynamite. When the bear came back, they blew it up—"raised that bear maybe four or five feet" in the air and smashed all its bones. And the little dog got his reward—the foreman kept him as a companion in the park for many years.

Mary's Bay, Yellowstone Lake. 1871
—W.H. Jackson photo, National Park Service, Yellowstone National Park.

Fishing Bridge—West Thumb

Chapter VII

Fishing Bridge to
West Thumb

21 Miles

The Lake Hotel
Mile 1.5 from Fishing Bridge
Mile 19.5 from West Thumb

The Lake Hotel rose here on the shore of Yellowstone Lake a century ago. In those early days it was one of the favored spots of the elegant carriage-trade folk. They were escorted around the park on pre-arranged tours in relative luxury, not merely eating but dining, sitting not on logs but in wingback chairs, and sleeping not on the ground but in hotel beds. They traveled in coaches, usually four-horse, eleven-passenger rigs. These coaches were driven by local men with names like Society Red, Cryin' Jack, Scattering Jesus, who was flighty, White Mountain Smith, and Geyser Bob, a spinner of yarns.

According to the Livingston, Montana, newspaper, Geyser Bob got his name from one of his tales:

"I clum up on Old Faithful one day and got too near the crater and fell in."

"How interesting!" commented the lady [a tourist]. "What happened?"

"Why," said Bob pointing to the Beehive Geyser across the Firehole River, "I came out of the Beehive—over there."

"Well! Well! How long did it take?"

"Oh," said Bob, "if I had come straight through it would have taken about ten minutes, but I stopped on the way for a haircut and a shave!"

Doubtless the lady understood that Bob was indulging in the time-honored Western sport of stuffing dudes, a descendant of the mountain-man love of yarning. One of the reasons dudes get stuffed, of course, is that they ask such remarkable questions. Discussions with park rangers and local guides, with strict promises of anonymity, yield such memorable dude questions as these:

"When do you plant the wildflowers?"
"What time of year do the elk change to moose?"
"What color uniforms do the cattle guards wear?"

One of the principal amusements at the Lake Hotel in the early days was watching the bears feed on hotel garbage. The Western novelist Owen Wister described one such episode of the 1890s:

I walked out once in the early evening at the Lake Hotel and counted twenty-one bears feasting. I saw a bear march up to a tourist and accept candy from his hand, while his wife stood at a safe distance, protesting vainly, but I think rightly. I saw the twenty-one bears suddenly cease feasting and withdraw to a short distance. Out of the trees came a true grizzly, long-snouted and ugly; and while he selected his dinner with ostentatious care and began to enjoy it, a cinnamon bear stole discreetly, as if on tip-toe, toward the meal he had left behind him. He got pretty near it, when the grizzly paused in eating and merely swung his head at him—no more than that; in a flash the cinnamon had galloped humpty-dumptily off and sat down watching. He came back presently; and the scene was re-enacted three times before I had enough of it and left; each time when the cinnamon had reached a certain point the grizzly swung his head, and this invariably sufficed. It is my notion that the cinnamon was a bit of a wag."

M-Y coach at Lake Hotel, ca 1900
—J.E. Haynes photo, Montana Historical Society.

On his visit to the park in 1903, President Theodore Roosevelt found the bear situation commendable:

The effect of protection upon bear life in the Yellowstone has been one of the phenomena of natural history. Not only have they grown to realize that they are safe, but, being natural scavengers and foul feeders, they have come to recognize the garbage heaps of the hotels as their special sources of food supply. Throughout the summer months they come to all the hotels in numbers, usually appearing in the late afternoon or evening, and they have become as indifferent to the presence of men as the deer themselves—some of them very much more indifferent. They have now taken their place among the recognized sights of the Park, and the tourists are nearly as much interested in them as in the geysers.

That last comment of TR's show how times have changed. Now it's rare to see a bear, and even a small black bear will draw a crowd. Roosevelt goes on:

It is curious to think that the descendants of the great grizzlies which were the dread of the early explorers and hunters should now be semi-domesticated creatures, boldly hanging around crowded hotels for the sake of what they can pick up, and quite harmless so long as any reasonable precaution is exercised....

At times the bears get so bold that they take to making inroads on the kitchen. One completely terrorized a Chinese cook. It would drive him off and then feast upon whatever was left behind. When a bear begins to act in this way or to show surliness it is sometimes necessary to shoot it. Other bears are tamed until they will feed out of the hand, and will come at once if called. Not only have some of the soldiers and scouts tamed bears in this fashion, but occasionally a chambermaid or waiter girl at one of the hotels has thus developed a bear as a pet.

But feeding the bears hotel garbage was a problem — people got hurt. The garbage dumps were closed in the early 1970s amid controversy. At the time, both the park administration and most independent researchers agreed that the dumps should be closed, both to increase human safety and to force the bears to return to natural sources of food. The grizzly researchers Frank and John Craighead, however, who had had other disagreements with the park administration, argued that the dumps should be phased out so that the bears would not be pushed into such an abrupt adjustment.

"The park was proceeding on the unfounded assumption," Frank Craighead now says, "that there were two grizzly bear populations, one of the backcountry and one at the dumps," and proposed to eliminate the dependent population in favor of the wild one. But the Craigheads said that there was no such distinction, that most of the bears visited the dumps at some point in their lives, so no wild population would remain.

Bears in vicinity of garbage dump near Fountain Hotel, Fountain Geyser Basin, August, 1897.
—C.D. Walcott photo, U.S. Geological Survey.

The dumps were closed all at once, and years of argument have ensued. "We said the bears would come back looking for food, get into the campgrounds, and there would be confrontations and loss of human life," says Frank Craighead. "What bothers them, I think, is that all of that has happened."

Some scientists now assert that Yellowstone should have garbage dumps, as modern equivalents of big sources of food that nature used to provide, such as buffalo carcasses where they ran off cliffs and died in herds.

Strict regulations now govern what the hotels do with their garbage, and what campers do with food.

Grizzlies still prowl some of the areas frequented by people, and that inevitably leads to bear-human conflict. In such incidents the people often get hurt or even killed first, and the bears later end up getting shot by the Park Service. Since the grizzlies are threatened in Yellowstone, every death is controversial.

The Park Service's mandate from Congress is to keep Yellowstone as close as possible to its original state of nature, which (in the Park Service interpretation) means neither feeding nor killing the bears. But some researchers and other observers, including Frank Craighead, author of *The Track of the Grizzly*, argue that keeping Yellowstone natural is a dream of the past. "You can't manage the park as a primeval area," says Craighead, "when it gets several million visitors a year."

Bridge Bay
Mile 3.5 from Fishing Bridge
Mile 17.5 from West Thumb

Here at Bridge Bay the boating entrepreneur E. C. Waters rented rowboats around the turn of the century. A customer found the charge of twelve dollars outrageous, and complained, "The only satisfaction I had was in telling him that I now knew why Christ walked on the water, that in the face of such charges anybody else would walk that was able to."

Waters got commercial boating started on Yellowstone Lake in 1889, when he launched the steamboat *Zillah* to carry passengers between the Lake Hotel and West Thumb. Waters ran this passenger service for twenty years, but finally grew too ambitious. In 1905 he built the *E. C. Waters*, a steamer capable of hauling 500 people, according to Waters. But park authorities would license it for only 125 passengers. Waters refused to operate under those terms, and moored the idle steamer on Stevenson Island, the large, timbered island opposite here. Two decades later the boilers were removed from the steamer to heat the Lake Hotel, and the remainder was burned.

Today commercial boats operate regularly from Bridge Bay.

Steamer Zillah *at dock, with E.C. Waters on the dock, 1904.*
—F.J. Haynes photo, Montana Historical Society

Yellowstone Lake etching.
—Montana Historical Society

Gull Point Drive
Mile 4 from Fishing Bridge
Mile 17 from West Thumb

Here a pleasant lakeshore drive turns off toward Gull Point, rejoining the Grand Loop Road two miles toward West Thumb. Somewhere along this north shore of Yellowstone Lake is the source of a favorite story attributed to the master mountain man Jim Bridger. Hot springs empty into the lake here, and hot water rises and stays on the surface. That's why Bridger used to brag about catching fish in the depths of the lake and cooking them in the hot water on the way out.

This north shore of the lake is thickly covered with lodgepole pine. They're easy to identify—tall, straight evergreens with branches only toward the top. The name comes from the use Indians found for them: These trees made long, slender, easily-trimmed poles for their buffalo-hide lodges.

The West Thumb Area

The Potts Geyser Basin was the source of the first published description of the park's thermal features, a letter by the mountain man Daniel Potts:

The Yellow-stone has a large fresh water Lake near its head on the verry top of the Mountain which is about one hundred by forty miles in diameter and as clear as a crystal on the south border of this lake is a number of hot and boiling springs some of water and others of most beautiful fine clay and resembles that of a mush pot and throws its particles to the immense height of twenty to thirty feet in height The clay is white and of a pink and water appears fathomless as it appears to be entirely hollow under neath. There is also a number of places where the pure suphor is sent forth in abundance one of our men Visited one of those wilst taking his recreation there at an instan the earth began a tremendious trembling and he with difficulty made his escape when an explosion took place resembling that of thunder. During our stay in that quarter I heard it every day.

Thumb Bay nearly brought disaster to the Doane expedition. In October of 1876 Lieutenant Gustavus Doane, who had served the Washburn expedition well, got orders to explore the Snake River from its source to its mouth at the Columbia River. He was to make the trip with one non-commissioned officer and five privates, a boat, and 60 days rations—in the autumn or winter, when travel in Yellowstone is dangerous.

The men built the boat, disassembled it so that it could be reassembled with wood screws, and packed the boat to Yellowstone Lake. Here they towed the boat along the shore, got swamped at Pumice Point, salvaged the cargo, and repaired the boat.

Here at Thumb Bay Doane directed three of the six men to row across. But they didn't appear on time, and a storm was rising. Just when Doane was giving them up for lost, he heard their "boisterous and double-jointed profanity." They made the shore safely, but their "hair and beards were frozen to their caps and overcoats and they were sheeted with glistening ice from head to foot."

From that point the expedition only fared worse. The men dragged the boat to Heart Lake and launched again, but found the streams not really navigable until the Lewis River entered the Snake. Through Jackson Hole they lived on fish and horsemeat, leading Doane to comment memorably that "the worn out U. S. Cavalry plug was never intended for food." In the canyon of the Snake below Jackson Hole, they wrecked the boat, and were obliged to walk to Fort Hall, Idaho, where the expedition was cancelled.

West Thumb —South Entrance

Chapter VIII

West Thumb to
South Entrance

21 miles

Grant Village
Mile 2 from West Thumb
Mile 19 from the south entrance

Grant Village was constructed in the late 1970s and early 1980s. Its original purpose was to replace facilities at Fishing Bridge, Old Faithful, and West Thumb. The Park Service wanted to provide camping away from primary resource areas to diminish the human pressure on them, and to reduce the number of people at Fishing Bridge, where they get into conflicts with the numerous grizzly bears. But closing any facilities at Fishing Bridge became a political issue, and now is in limbo. Nor were facilities closed at the other locations. Instead a sizeable quarrel has erupted between those who emphasize making the park accessible and those who emphasize preserving it, with the Park Service caught in the middle.

The burns visible around Grant Village and further south on this stretch of road were left by one of the historic fires of 1988, the Red Fire. This was one of the early fires caused by lightning that at first was allowed to burn unsuppressed. After it was being fought, it joined the Shoshone,

Falls, and Mink fires to make what was called the Snake River Complex, threatening Grant Village, the Lewis Lake campground, and on some days closing the road to the south entrance.

For a fuller report on the wildfires of 1988 and a discussion of the park's fire policies, see pp. 90-94.

Lake Soldier's Station
—National Park Service, Yellowstone National Park

Lewis Lake
Miles 8-9 from West Thumb
Miles 12-13 from the south entrance

Here the road follows the eastern shore of Lewis Lake, named for Meriwether Lewis, one of the co-captains of the

Lewis and Clark expedition, which explored the West from St. Louis to the Pacific Ocean and back from 1803 to 1806. The expedition never came into the wonderland that is now Yellowstone National Park, but on the return journey William Clark did go down the lower Yellowstone River.

The Lewis River
Miles 11-17 from West Thumb
Miles 4-10 from the south entrance

The Lewis River, whose beautiful bottoms and dramatic canyon the road follows through this area, was also named for Meriwether Lewis.

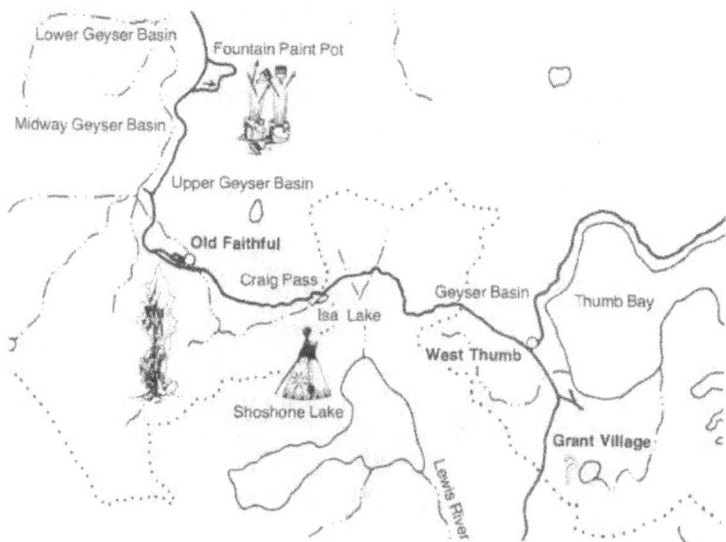

West Thumb—Old Faithful

Chapter IX
West Thumb to
Old Faithful Area

18 miles

The road between West Thumb and Old Faithful, which crosses the continental divide twice, was built in 1891 under the direction of Hiram M. Chittenden, then lieutenant of the Army Corps of Engineers. Chittenden was generally judged to have performed superbly in a difficult task of route-finding and construction in rugged country. (But the modern road does not use his route entirely.) Chittenden later wrote the first comprehensive history of the park, *The Yellowstone National Park* (1895 and several other editions), a prime source for every subsequent writer about Yellowstone.

Shoshone Point
Mile 9.5 from West Thumb
Mile 8.5 from Old Faithful

At Shoshone Point one of the park's infamous stage robberies took place in July of 1914. It was still the era of the carriage-trade travelers, ladies and gentlemen of means who took the grand tour of the park in style. (Automobiles would shortly put an end to the stagecoach days.) The drivers customarily stopped at Shoshone Point to let the tourists take in the grand view of Shoshone Lake and the distant Tetons.

On this particular day a man in a black kerchief held a rifle on the passengers of the first coach and ordered them to put their cash and jewelry on his blanket. One at a time, fifteen coaches drove up, and the kerchiefed man robbed them all. He was not strict, though, and even hinted that a couple of young ladies could hide their pretty baubles in their pretty stockings, which they did. This bit of style, and other quips, got him the nickname the Merry Bandit. He was not strict in other ways either—he didn't notice that three tourists took photographs of him, and a preacher even made a sketch. The bandit collected altogether only about a thousand dollars worth of valuables, which may indicate that the fancy folk were traveling with smaller means than their appearances indicated.

The pictures and other evidence soon led the authorities to a ranch in Idaho on the trail of a poacher, ex-convict and general rogue named Edward B. Trafton. He was sentenced to five years in the federal penitentiary at Leavenworth, Kansas.

Trafton later claimed to have been the model for a famous Western literary character, Trampas in *The Virginian*. But novelist Owen Wister did not verify that claim.

Craig Pass and Isa Lake
Mile 10.5 from West Thumb
Mile 7.5 from Old Faithful

Craig Pass, at the top of the continental divide, was named for the first lady to cross it on the new road engineered by Hiram Chittenden, one Ida Craig. In the pass on both sides of the road is a geological rarity, Isa Lake, which, as the interpretive sign explains, drains into both the Atlantic and Pacific watersheds. So does Two Ocean Creek, south of the park. Tales of waters that divided toward both the Atlantic and Pacific got mountain men like the old master Jim Bridger into trouble. Surely such a thing was impossible! said experts of the day. But the trapper Osborne Russell had described it in his journal in the 1830s:

> On the South side about midway of the prairie stands a high snowy peak from which issues a stream of water which, after entering the plain it divides equally, one half running West and the other East, thus bidding adieu to each other; one bound for the Pacific and the other for the Atlantic Ocean. Here a trout of 12 inches may cross the Mountains in safety. Poets have sung of the "meeting of the waters" and the fish climbing cataracts but the "parting of the waters" and the fish crossing mountains I believe remains unsung as yet by all except the solitary Trapper who sits under the shade of a spreading pine whistling blank-verse and beating time to the tune with a whip on his trap sack.

Isa Lake
—J.E. Haynes, Montana Historical Society

A Stage Holdup
Mile 16 from West Thumb
Mile 2 from Old Faithful

Somewhere in this area, at what was called Turtle Rock, what may have been the biggest stagecoach robbery of the twentieth century took place in August of 1908. Still, the amount taken was modest, a little over two thousand dollars.

Twenty-five vehicles came up the road from Old Faithful, some coaches of the companies that offered grand tours via hotels, some wagons of the Wylie Company, which put its guests up in permanent tent camps. The robber let the first eight coaches pass to let the escorting cavalryman get well up the road, and then stopped the next eight coaches as they came up and made the passengers put their valuables in a bag. Then he waited for the nine Wylie wagons and did the same.

Though the alarm was sounded quickly by telephone, the robber was never caught.

The park suffered five stagecoach robberies altogether—the first in Gardner Canyon in 1887, the second on the road between Canyon and Norris in 1897, this one in 1908, the fourth southeast of here at Shoshone Point in 1914, and the last, which also may have been the last in the United States, near Madison Junction in 1915.

The Old Faithful Area, Upper Geyser Basin

The geysers and hot springs of the Upper Geyser Basin along the Firehole River are certainly among the wonders of the world and probably got their white-man discovery by a brigade of mountain men led by Manuel Alvarez in 1833. That summer they told Warren Angus Ferris, a clerk with the American Fur Company, about the thermal miracles, and the next May Ferris left his trapping brigade with two Pend' Oreille Indians and journeyed to the Firehole to see the miracles for himself. His immediate response was that he might have exclaimed with the Queen of Sheba, when their full reality of dimensions and novelty burst upon his view, "The half was not told me."

From the surface of a rocky plain or table, burst forth columns of water, of various dimensions, projected high in the air, accompanied by loud explosions, and sulphurous vapors, which were highly disagreeable to the smell.... The largest of these wonderful fountains, projects a column of boiling water several feet in diameter, to the height of more than one hundred and fifty feet, ... accompanied with a tremendous noise. These explosions and discharges occur at intervals of about two hours [Ferris is probably speaking of Splendid Geyser]. After having witnessed three of them, I ventured near enough to put my hand into the water of its basin, but withdrew it instantly, for the heat of the water in this immense cauldron, was altogether too great for comfort, and the agitation of the water, the disagreeable effluvium continually exuding, and the hollow unearthly rumbling under the rock on which I stood, so ill accorded with my notions of personal safety, that I retreated back precipitately to a respectful distance. The Indians who were with me, were quite appalled, and could not by any means be induced to approach them. They seemed astonished at my presumption in advancing up to the large one, and when I safely returned, congratulated me on my "narrow escape." — They believed them to be supernatural, and supposed them to be the production of the Evil Spirit. One of them remarked that hell, of which he had heard from the whites, must be in the vicinity.

The Upper Basin Soldier Station
—Haynes Studio, Montana Historical Society

Not everyone had so ecstatic a response to the geysers as
Ferris. Consider, for instance, the reactions of some tourists
whom British master story-teller Rudyard Kipling observed:

> I have been through the Yellowstone National Park
> in a buggy, in the company of an adventurous old lady
> from Chicago and her husband, who disapproved of
> scenery as being 'ungodly.' I fancy it scared them ....
> The old lady, ... regarding the horrors of the fire-holes,
> could only say, "Good Lord!" at thirty-second intervals. Her
> husband talked about "dreffel waste of steam-power ...."
> "What I say," shrieked the old lady apropos of mat-
> ters theological, ... "after having seen all that, is that the
> Lord has ordained a Hell for such as disbelieve his gra-
> cious works ...."
> "And if," continued the old lady, "if we find a thing so
> dreffel as all that steam and sulphur allowed on the face
> of the earth, mustn't we believe that there is something

ten-thousand times more terrible below prepared untoe our destruction?"

"Now I shall be able to say something to Anna Fincher about her way of living. Sha'n't I, Blake?" This to her husband.

Surprisingly, the naturalist John Burroughs, who toured the park with his friend President Theodore Roosevelt in 1903, was likewise negative:

> The novelty of the geyser region soon wears off. Steam and hot water are steam and hot water the world over, and the exhibition of them here did not differ, except in volume, from what one sees by his own fireside. The 'Growler' is only a boiling tea-kettle on a large scale, and 'Old Faithful' is as if the lid were to fly off, and the whole contents of the kettle should be thrown high into the air. To be sure, boiling lakes and steaming rivers are not common, but the new features seemed, somehow, out of place, and as if nature had made a mistake.

Of course, people are understandably afraid of geysers. The Western illustrator Frederic Remington rode horseback through a thermal area with some army companions, and judged the deed reckless because the ground "is very thin and hazardous, and to break through is to be boiled. One instinctively objects to that form of cooking."

A bicyclist adventurous enough to tour the park on a two-wheeler in 1883, W. O. Owen, was also brave enough to get in trouble via the geysers:

> Abrilliant idea seized me that a cup of tea made from boiling geyser water would be something to boast

of at home. Accordingly the teapot was filled with geyser liquid, a handful of tea thrown in and in a few minutes the mixture was declared ready for use. The idea was so romantic and unusual that nothing short of three cups of this delightful beverage would appease me, although my [two] companions were prudent enough to be satisfied with a much less quantity. In less than an hour I was visited with an attack of seasickness that even now makes me shudder to recall. The most violent retching and blinding headache, accompanied with vertigo, were the prevailing symptoms; and for a short time it seemed that one-third of the bicycle party would find a resting place in the Upper Geyser Basin.

Old Faithful Geyser and three bicyclists, Sept. 1895
—F.J. Haynes photo, Montana Historical Society

Some of the early park visitors thought the geysers would make marvelous natural washing machines, and put them to the test. A Livingston, Montana, newspaperman, blissfully unaware that his words might later offend Americans of Chinese descent, told this story of a Chinese laundryman:

It is written in the Archives of Yellowstone Park that a child of the Flowery Kingdom, wearing the usual smile on his childlike face, and his shirt outside his trousers, came to the Upper Geyser Basin to establish a laundry, because there was enough hot water there to run a Presidential Campaign. He pitched his tent over a thermal Spring, wrote his name in wierd characters upon a sign board, and when the raiments of the native and pilgrim came in, he chucked the whole invoice into the bubbling spring. Then he threw in a bar of soap, and smiled to see the great forces that upheave mountains and shake continents, and toss the mighty Globe into convulsions most awful, doing plain washing in a Chinese laundry. But the spring was a slumbering geyser. The soap awakened the imprisoned giant; with a roar that made the earth tremble, and a shriek of a steam whistle, a cloud of steam and a column of boiling water shot up into the air a hundred feet, carrying soap, raiment, tent and Chinaman along with the rush, and dropping them at various intervals along the way. "Hookee-la," said John, when he came down—way down! "Joss he no like washee for China-boy. Too muchee bubblee make." And since that day men have known the way to arouse a slumbering geyser is to give the monster soap.

Chinaman Spring, near Old Faithful, got its name from this incident.

Later Owen Wister, who was made famous by his Western novel *The Virginian*, reported that doing laundry in geysers had become popular, but that it is not true that there was "a hole into which you could toss your soiled handkerchief and have it disappear and in a minute be thrown out washed, ironed, folded, and with a laundry mark."

Wister tried doing laundry himself:

> We steep the garment in a quiet blue pool, deep, and shaped exactly like a great calla lily, filled to the brim and some ten feet across. Then we soap and then with a pole poke it down a spluttering crevice that foams all over it until it is ready to take out and dry....
>
> But to soap a geyser is very bad for it; disturbs its rhythm, dislocates its circulation, and makes it play when it isn't due to play, has killed one important geyser, I have heard.

Chinaman Geyser "soaped"
—F.J. Haynes photo, Montana Historical Society

Old Faithful Inn and coaches
—Haynes Studio, Montana Historical Society

That's why the army banned soaping. In 1888 two railroad officials took a tour of the park, guided by Yellowstone Park Association general manager E. C. Waters, who would later initiate commercial boating on Yellowstone Lake. Waters soaped Beehive Geyser for the railroad bigwigs—and they got arrested. Livingston newspaper correspondent Bob Burdet, glad to get a geyser exhibition paid for by someone else, quipped, "Don't tell me that a railroad president isn't good for something."

Wister reports that, though the army took its duty to protect the geysers seriously, it could show compassion.

A soldier at the Upper [Geyser] Basin had reported a clergyman as having broken off a bagful of formation. [Captain] Edwards found him seated in the stage, about to depart from the Fountain.

"You have taken no specimens of course?"

"No."

"You give me your word as a preacher of the Gospel that you have nothing of the sort in that bag?"

"I do."

Edwards let him go.

"But why?" I asked.

"I couldn't humiliate a minister in front of the crowd."

Old Faithful Inn, built in 1904 and called the largest log structure in the world, was designed by Seattle architect Robert C. Reamer, who also designed the gateway arch at the north entrance. One-time Park Service historian Aubrey Haines, author of *The Yellowstone Story*, says, "The lobby was the focus of Mr. Reamer's rustic effect. It is a great, balconied cavern, open to the roof, with all supporting beams and braces exposed to view like the skeleton of some enormous mammal seen from within. In one corner is a mighty fireplace with its chimney exposed to the point where it passes through the ridge 85 feet above the floor…, containing, in all, 500 tons of stone taken from a quarry site five miles to the east. The fireplace chimney is faced with a giant clock hammered out by a blacksmith named Colpitts, who also made the distinctive hardware."

Old Faithful Inn Chimney and stairways. 1904.
—F.J. Haynes. Montana Historical Society

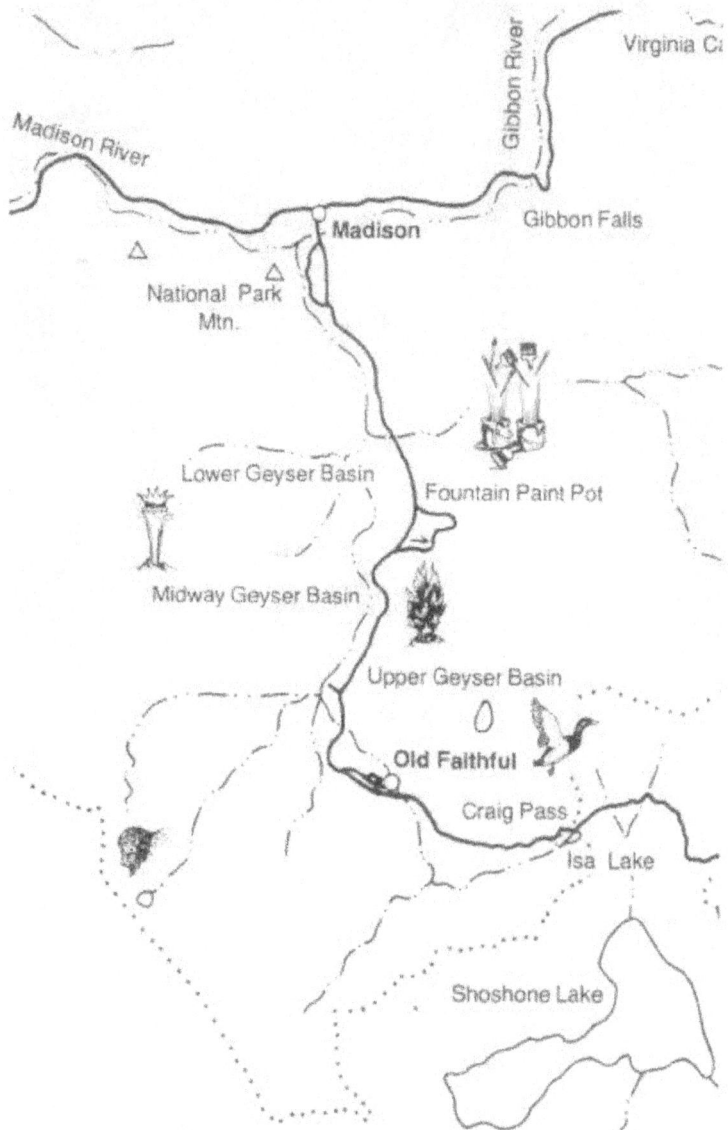

Old Faithful—Madison Junction

CHAPTER X
OLD FAITHFUL TO MADISON JUNCTION

16 miles

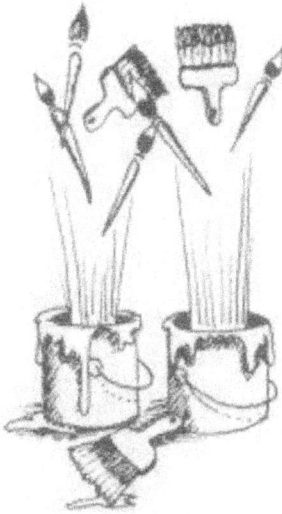

Midway Geyser Basin
Mile 7 from Old Faithful
Mile 9 from Madison Junction

Thermal phenomena like these in Midway Geyser Basin led the naturalist John Muir to reach an odd conclusion about a repugnant substance, mud:

These valleys at the heads of the great rivers may be regarded as laboratories and kitchens, in which, amid a thousand retorts and pots, we may see Nature at work as chemist or cook, cunningly compounding an infinite variety of mineral messes; cooking whole mountains; boiling and steaming flinty rocks to smooth paste and mush,—yellow, brown, red, pink, lavender, gray, and creamy white,—making the most beautiful mud in the world; and distilling the most ethereal essences.

Fountain Hotel, 1890.
—F.J. Haynes Photo, Montana Historical Society

Lower Geyser Basin
Mile 8.5 from Old Faithful
Mile 7.5 from Madison Junction

The Fountain Hotel, here in Lower Geyser Basin, built in 1891, was where bears were first fed hotel garbage. Black bears would come every evening, while guests watched from as little as ten yards away, or even fed the bears from their hands. This practice led to the well-known problems of later years, so that garbage must now be disposed of under close regulation, campers' handling of food is strictly controlled, and bears are a comparatively rare sight.

Some campers had difficulties with bears and food even at the turn of the century, as this German tourist did when a bear stole a ham from his grub box in the middle of the night:

> Och, I vas so mad, I say I go mit club and kill dat bear, but mine pardner, he vas old bear man; he say, "No, Fritz, dat bear have got hog's ham. You go mit a stick for him he got your ham." So I leaved dat d— bear sit on him tail and chew, vile I cuss him til daylight comes.

The journalist Charles Dudley Warner tells about a lunch-station keeper who got so well acquainted with a she-bear that she:

> ... used to come to his house every day and walk into the kitchen for food for herself and her two cubs. The cubs never came. The keeper got on very intimate terms with the bear, who was always civil and well-behaved, and would take food from his hand (without taking the hand). One day toward sunset the bear came to the kitchen, and having received her portion, she went out

of the back door to carry it to her cubs. To her surprise and anger, the cubs were there waiting for her. She laid down the food, and rushed at her infants and gave them a rousing spanking. "She did not cuff them; she spanked them," and then she drove them back into the woods, cuffing them and knocking them at every step. When she reached the spot where she had told them to wait, she left them there and returned to the house. And there she stayed in the kitchen for two whole hours, making the disobedient children wait for their food, simply to discipline them and teach them obedience. The explanation is very natural. When the bear leaves her young in a particular place and goes in search of food for them, if they stray away in her absence she has great difficulty in finding them. The mother knew that the safety of her cubs and her own peace of mind depended upon strict discipline in the family. O that we had more such mothers in the United States!

Bears feeding 'a la carte,' eating from the back of a horse-drawn garbage wagon.
—E.W. Hunter photo, Montana Historical Society

The Nez Perce War
Mile 11 from Old Faithful
Mile 5 from Madison Junction

Nez Perce Creek is the area of one of the few conflicts between whites and Indians in the park, a minor event of the Nez Perce War, as a park interpretive sign here explains.

Some non-treaty Nez Perce (the name is generally pronounced in the West like *fez purse*, not *Nay Pairsay* in the French fashion) had been roaming their old hunting grounds, and in 1877 the government tried to put them on the reservation by force—and precipitated a war.

Led by Chief Joseph, 600 Nez Perces fled eastward, fighting a running engagement with the U. S. Army. In late August they entered Yellowstone National Park via Targhee Pass, pursued by 600 soldiers under the command of General Oliver O. Howard. Before long they came on a prospector, and a party of ordinary tourists from Montana.

The Nez Perces took all the whites into captivity, destroyed some tourist wagons, and arbitrarily traded their own poor horses for the tourists'.

Mrs. George Cowan, one of the tourists, had to give up her good mount, and later wrote about the trade:

> It occurs to me at this writing that the above mode of trading is a fair reflection of the lesson taught by whites. For instance, a tribe of Indians are located on a reservation. Gold is discovered thereon by some prospector. A stampede follows. The strong arm of the government alone prevents the avaricious pale face from possessing himself of the land forthwith. Soon negotiations are pending with as little delay as a few yards of red tape will permit. A treaty is signed, the strip ceded to the government and opened to settlers and "Lo, the poor Indian" finds himself on a tract a few degrees more arid, a little less desirable than his former home. The Indian has few rights the average white settler feels bound to respect.

Though she may not have known it, Mrs. Cowan hit on the exact case here. In 1855 the government and the Nez Perces had agreed on a reservation in the country where the modern states Idaho, Washington, and Oregon meet. Five years later a gold rush brought whites onto Indian lands illegally. A treaty soon ceded these lands to the whites, reducing the reservation. But certain Nez Perce leaders, including Joseph, refused to sign the treaty or to restrict themselves to this smaller reservation, thus bringing on the war.

After the forced horse trade with Mrs. Cowan and the others, the Nez Perces turned the tourists loose. One Indian, though, Poker Joe, warned them to ride fast to avoid the wrath of the more unruly Nez Perces. Soon shooting broke out, and two of the whites were wounded. Mrs. Cowan, seeing her husband George shot in the head, fainted, and later assumed he was dead. But Cowan regained consciousness, got shot again in the side as he tried to escape, dragged himself into the forest, and survived. The rest of the party was likewise scattered in the forest, or recaptured.

That night Mrs. Cowan camped with Joseph. She wrote later of him, "The chief sat by the fire, sombre and silent, foreseeing in his gloomy meditations possibly the unhappy ending of his campaign. The 'noble red man' we read of was more nearly impersonated in this Indian than in any I have ever met. Grave and dignified, he looked a chief."

After crossing the Yellowstone River at Nez Perce Ford, which is known to the world unofficially as Buffalo Ford, the Indians released the Montana tourists, who found their way back to the oncoming soldiers and the good news that their comrades were alive. The next day, though, some of the Nez Perces shot up the camp of some other tourists from Montana at the forks of Otter Creek, and those white men had to take to the woods—one was later found dead of a gunshot wound.

The spread-out Nez Perce continued to flee toward the eastern border of the park, on the way burning Baronett Bridge and doing some raiding in the Yellowstone Valley outside the park, where another white man was killed, and along the Lamar River. Then, after two weeks in wonderland, the Indians passed out of Yellowstone National Park.

Chief Joseph.
—D.F. Barry photo, University of Montana Archives

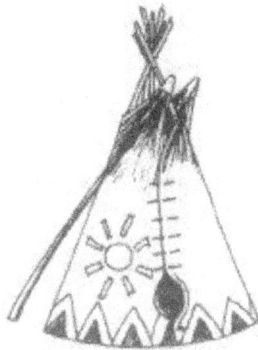

Joseph then led his people north toward Canada. General Nelson Miles intercepted them in the Bear Paw Mountains and brought an end to the rebellion on Snake Creek, about 30 miles from the Canadian border.

The Nez Perce War had lasted three months and 22 days. The flight and pursuit covered over 1500 miles. At least fifteen engagements were fought. White casualties were six officers killed and thirteen wounded, 121 soldiers and citizens killed and 127 wounded. Nez Perce casualties were at least 151 killed, 88 wounded, and 489 captured. The Nez Perce, for their efforts, won only the admiration of many other Americans. The historian Hiram Chittenden wrote of their war:

> This celebrated campaign is well intended to elicit the fullest sympathy for the unfortunate Nez Perces. They had always been a friendly tribe and it was their boast that they had never slain a white man. They were intelligent, brave, and humane. In this campaign they bought supplies which they might have confiscated; they saved property which they might have destroyed; they spared hundreds of lives which other Indians would have sacrificed. Their conduct places them nearer the standard of civilized people than any other of the native tribes of the continent.

The next year, 1878, saw more Indian-white skirmishes in the park, a minor siege of troubles known as the Bannock War, and with that red-white warfare in Yellowstone was finished. By 1883, just six years after the high tragedy of the Nez Perce War, run-ins between Indians and whites had turned to high comedy. W. O. Owen and two companions encountered Indians unexpectedly when they were making, incredibly, the first bicycle tour of the park.

> By severe pedaling the top [of the continental divide, probably at Targhee Pass] was reached, when, throwing legs over handles, we began our first coast and flew down the mountain with the speed of the wind. Some distance ahead we observed a large, moving body

square in the road, coming our way, but with all our eyes we could not satisfy our minds as to what it might be. At the speed we were going, however, the distance was soon sufficiently shortened to explain the matter, and we ascertained that it was a number of Indians traveling west. Here was a predicament indeed, and how to extricate ourselves was the next problem demanding speedy solution. We had no means of knowing whether these Americans were peaceable or on the warpath, and, fearing it might be the latter, it was deemed best to make a rush and frighten them before they could realize what was in the wind ….

In my heart I believe that no men ever moved with greater velocity on a wheel than did we on this occasion. We dashed into their midst at a speed which I dare not even conjecture, and, with the most unearthly yells that ever reached human ears, squaws, chiefs, horses and innumerable dogs scattered in as many directions as there are points to the mariner's compass. It was a desperate charge, but entirely successful, and, passing the Indians, we reached the foot of the hill in safety.

The Madison Junction Area

The museum at Madison Junction is a National Historic Landmark as an example of Rustic Architecture.

Legend has it that the idea of turning the Yellowstone wonderland into the first national park got its real beginning right here. In a camp virtually in the shadow of National Park Mountain, the timbered summit to the southwest, the members of the Washburn expedition were lounging around the fire and talking of all that they had seen—this was their first camp since coming from the geyser basins just up the Firehole River. The date was September 19, 1870. The tale is that it was an evening when the spirit of generosity would overcome the impulse toward acquisitiveness. According to historian Hiram Chittenden, someone remarked what an:

> ... important pleasure resort so wonderful a region must soon become .... It was suggested that it would be a "profitable speculation" to take up land around the various objects of interest. The conversation had not proceeded far on these lines when one of the party, Cornelius Hedges, interposed and said that private ownership of that region, or any part of it, ought never to be countenanced; but that it ought to be set apart by the government and forever held to the unrestricted use of the people. This higher view of the subject found immediate acceptance with the other members of the party. It was agreed that the project should be at once set afoot and pushed vigorously to a finish.

Even if this conversation took place as stated, it was not the first suggestion that the Yellowstone country should be a park reserved for all the people. Earlier ones came from Thomas Meagher, the acting governor of Montana Territory, in 1865, and from David Folsom, after he went exploring in the park in 1869.

After that important campfire discussion, one of the Washburn men, Nathaniel Langford, who later became the first superintendent of the park, gave a series of lectures in the East about the Yellowstone country on behalf of the Northern Pacific Railroad, which already saw Yellowstone as a potential focus of tourism; Langford later claimed to have put forward the national park idea in these lectures.

In 1871 Dr. Ferdinand Hayden led a government survey-ing expedition through the park, and then became a prime mover in pushing the park legislation through Congress. On March 1, 1872, the act of dedication was signed, setting Yellowstone "apart as a public park and pleasuring ground for the benefit and enjoyment of the people," and providing "for the preservation from injury or spoliation of all timber, mineral deposits, natural curiosities or wonders with said park, and their retention in their natural condition."

Visitors wading in water of Great Fountain Geyser.
—National Park Service, Yellowstone National Park

CHAPTER XI

MADISON JUNCTION TO

WEST ENTRANCE

14 miles

This road along the Madison River, which is one of the three forks of the Missouri River, follows the approximate route of the trail into the park area used by the mountain men. But for some years after the time of this writing, late in 1988, the road may seem most conspicuous for glimpses of burns left by the North Fork Fire, the largest of that year's epochal wildfires.

The North Fork Fire was started July 22 by a wood cutter's cigarette outside the park. Despite immediate efforts at suppression, it was not contained until October. Before it was contained, it roared over more than half a million acres, actually burning about 385,000. It threatened the developments at Old Faithful, Madison Junction, and Norris, the town of West Yellowstone, Montana, park headquarters at Mammoth, Canyon, and even Tower-Roosevelt Lodge—so it ranged all the way from outside Yellowstone on the southwest border into the northeastern region of the park.

An odd result of this fire was the uncovering of the wreckage of a B-17 bomber that crashed in Jack Straw Basin in the spring of 1943, killing 10 airmen, a site that had been overgrown and almost forgotten by the public. In 1988 cleanup crews hauled out more than twelve tons of refuse, including bullets, a wing tip, small bits of clothing and equipment, and parts of practice bombs. The main hulk of the plane, covered by the rescue crews 45 years ago, was left in place.

Madison Junction — West Entrance

Forty-five years after the crash, its cause remained unknown. The plane was returning from California to its base in Lewiston, Montana, when it went down. One soldier parachuted out and survived.

The wildfires of 1988 uncovered a lot of other park ghosts as well—old road cuts, bridges, culverts, and sites of former garbage dumps. Heavy growth had made them hard to get to and expensive to remove. Park workers were busily cleaning up such left-overs in the fall of 1988, subject to determination that they didn't have historic value.

For a fuller history of the fires of 1988, and of park policy about fires, see pp. 90-94.

Madison Junction—Norris Junction

CHAPTER XII

MADISON JUNCTION TO
NORRIS JUNCTION

14 miles

The Gibbon River, which runs along this section of road, is named for Colonel John Gibbon, who led a detachment of soldiers into Yellowstone in 1871. The survey party of Dr. Ferdinand Hayden found the soldiers starving and gave them flour and sugar. The soldiers had come down this river (which here joins the Firehole River to form the Madison River), eating nothing but roots, squirrels, and jays.

The Area of Norris Junction

This junction, the geyser basin, Mount Norris, Norris Pass, and the Norris Museum are named for one of Yellowstone's great characters and the park's second superintendent (from 1877 to 1882), Philetus W. Norris.

Norris was occasionally a figure to poke fun at during his own time. A Bozeman newspaper, for instance, was waggish about his romantic appearance:

> A broad-brimmed white hat, looped up at the side and decorated with an eagle's feather. Long white hair reached far down upon his brawny shoulders; a white waving beard ornamented his breast. He wore a buckskin

hunting shirt, decked with long, flowing fringe. He wore a belt full of cartridges, and had a revolver hanging at his side. He also carried a hunting knife. He swung a tomahawk in his hand. He rode a gallant steed.

Roads 32 mi.; Trails 108 mi.   Roads 153 mi.; Trails 204 mi.

Development of Roads and Trails in Yellowstone National Park, 1877–1881
—from Aubrey Haines, *The Yellowstone Story*,
courtesy of The Yellowstone Association

The same writer had a little fun with Norris's inclination to name park features after himself:

Take the Norris wagon road and follow down the Norris fork of the Firehole River to the Norris Canyon of the Norris Obsidian Mountain; then go on to Mount Norris, on the summit of which you will find Monument Park of the Norris Blowout, and at its northerly base the Norris Basin and Park. Further on you will come to the Norris Geyser plateau and must not fail to see Geyser Norris. The Norris Falls of the Gibbon are worth a visit. The next point of interest is the Gibbon, half a day's ride from the Norris Hot Springs.

Despite his flamboyant style, Norris was an enterprising and effective superintendent at a time when the park needed one badly. He accomplished a feat of road-building that seems heroic: In the summer of 1878 he built a road of 60 miles from Mammoth to the Firehole River geyser basins in less than a month—without having a prior survey of the route, and under the disadvantage of his men having to guard themselves at all times against the rebellious Indians of the Bannock War. The park's first major historian, Hiram Chittenden, sums up Norris,

> He was an untiring explorer. He traveled all the existing trails and penetrated the unfrequented sections in every direction. He studied the history and antiquities of the Park. He built the first roads, opening a vast extent of highway, and although this has all been replaced by later work, it served its original purpose very well. He wrote and published a great deal about the Park and helped revive public interest in it at the time of its greatest need.

Norris Geyser Basin

The geyser basin named after Norris is one of the strange places of the earth, as British man of letters Rudyard Kipling observed on his trip here in 1889:

> We walked chattering to the uplands of Hell. They call it the Norris Geyser Basin on Earth. It was as though the tide of desolation had gone out, but would presently return, across innumerable acres of dazzling white geyser formation. There were no terraces here, but all other horrors. Not ten yards from the road a blast of steam shot up roaring every few seconds, a mud volcano spat

filth to Heaven, streams of hot water rumbled under foot, plunged through the dead pines in steaming cataracts and died on a waste of white where green-grey, black-yellow, and pink pools roared, shouted, bubbled, or hissed as their wicked fancies prompted. By the look of the eye the place should have been frozen over. By the feel of the feet it was warm. I ventured out among the pools, carefully following tracks, but one unwary foot began to sink, a squirt of water followed, and having no desire to descend quick into Tophet I returned to the shore where the mud and the sulphur and the nameless fat ooze-vegetation of Lethe lay. But the very road rang as though built over a gulf; and besides, how was I to tell when the raving blast of steam would find its vent insufficient and blow the whole affair into Nirvana?

In those days Norris Lunch Station was here, and managed by Lawrence Francis Mathews, an Irishman endowed with the gift of gab. Kipling dined at "Larry's," and paid a stiff price for canned beef, biscuits, and beer, but the Irishman's eloquence made it seem "imperial bounty."

Larry Matthews on the porch of his lunch station at Norris Geyser Basin, 1904.
—National Park Service, Yellowstone National Park

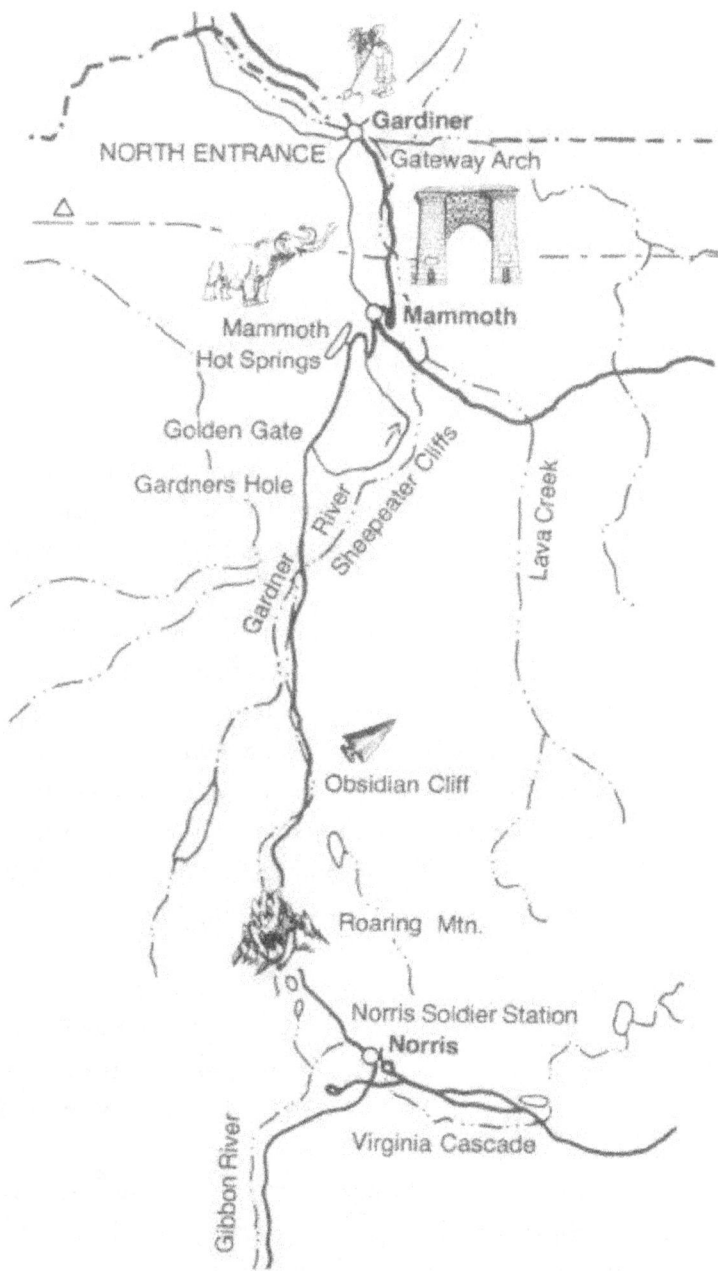

Norris Junction—Mammoth

Chapter XIII
Norris Junction to
Mammoth

21 miles

Norris Soldier Station
0.5 miles from Norris Junction
20.5 miles from Mammoth

N orris Soldier Station is one of three remaining soldier stations in the park, the others being at Tower Junction and Bechler. During the three decades of military administration, these buildings housed enlisted men away from park headquarters. Men stationed here during the long winters had contact with other human beings only via "Norwegian snowshoes"—what we would now call cross-country skis. They did regular patrols, even in winter, to help control poaching of big game.

Frying Pan Spring
2.5 miles from Norris Junction
18.5 miles from Mammoth

Frying Pan Spring, on the west side of the road, formerly called the Devil's Frying Pan, got its name from the bubbles that rise to the surface of the water as grease sizzles on a griddle. Former Park Service historian Aubrey Haines says in amusement that the park guides used to give out "a cock-and-bull story about how the birds in that locality drank so much hot water they all laid hard-boiled eggs, and anybody who didn't believe it could look in the woods roundabout, where the trees were full of nests containing just such eggs."

Tall tales like that one are a time-honored Western tradition, which visitors don't always catch on to right away. That champeen yarner and mountain man Jim Bridger, for instance, told one about the winter it snowed 70 days and 70 nights without stopping. The snow got 70 feet deep on the level. Herds upon herds of buffler froze standing up. Come the thaw, Bridger's men skinned 'em, rolled 'em into the Salt Lake, and pickled 'em. Made meat for themselves and the whole Shoshone nation for ten years, they did.

Roaring Mountain
Mile 5 from Norris Junction
Mile 16 from Mammoth

Roaring Mountain, the hill on the east side of the road, which still vents steam prodigiously, used to give off an eerie roaring sound as well.

The North Fork Fire
Mile 8 from Norris Junction
Mile 13 from Mammoth

The next ten miles of roadside show intermittent patterns of burn from 1988s largest wildfire, the North Fork Fire (which included the Wolf Lake Fire), a man-caused conflagration that started outside the southwest border of Yellowstone on

Map of the Yellowstone fires as of September, 1988. Over 1.1 million acres in Yellowstone National Park have been affected by fire. However only about half of the vegetation has burned within many of the fire perimeters shown.
—Source: Greater Yellowstone Post-Fire Resource Assessment Committee, Burned Area Survey Team

July 22, and scorched its way beyond Mammoth Hot Springs on the north and beyond Tower Junction to the northeast area of the park. It encircled about 560,000 acres, and burned nearly 500,000, more than half of the total burned inside the park during that ferocious fire season.

Since it was started by man, this fire was fought from its beginning. But some fires caused by lightning were only monitored at first, and later proved uncontrollable. The park's policy of letting some fires burn now has become hugely controversial, and according to park spokesmen is widely misunderstood.

Since 1972, along with some other national parks, Yellowstone has followed a policy of permitting natural fire to be a part of the park's basic wild processes. According to park researchers and other scientists, fire is an essential natural element in the park. It sweeps the grasslands in the northern part of the park several times in every hundred years, and the lodgepole forests of the central and southern park several times every thousand years.

Yellowstone's managers argue that fire does the park lots of good—it increases plant diversity and provides more food for lots of Yellowstone's animals. It does this by releasing more nutrients in the soil, encouraging the growth of smaller plants, and providing more light to the ground-level plants. Mature forests tend to shut out other plants, and fire helps to give the park tree stands of varying ages.

The managers also argue that fire has always played a role in the park region. It must continue to do that, they say, if the park is to be what park managers call an authentic vignette of primitive America.

To let fire do its historic job, the park's policy is to let lightning-caused fires burn when they don't threaten crucial values like human life, property, endangered species, and park boundaries, to suppress all fires caused by man, and to burn some areas deliberately.

Some observers think that the fires of 1988 proved this policy a failure. The summer turned out to be the driest in recorded park history, making the forests particularly vulnerable to fire. When the park administration did not fight some small fires from the outset, they became huge cataclysms, as did many of the fires that were fought from the beginning.

The critics of the natural-fire policy include some members of the media, many businessmen near the park, and even U.S. congressmen. Some of them contend merely that the park managers ought to follow their policy more flexibly and respond more quickly to exceptional circumstances like those of the summer of 1988. Others are dubious about any natural-fire policy at all, and argue for vigorous suppression of all fires or for prescribed burns that do the job of natural fire.

Park officials and many scientists and environmentalists answer that fire does have a historic role in the park, that cataclysmic fires in Yellowstone are a periodic event that cannot and should not be stopped, that burning is fundamentally good for the park, and that fighting the fires with bulldozers and other heavy equipment can sometimes be more destructive to the environment than fire itself.

As of this writing, debates about fire policy are going on at the highest levels of the the Congress and the National Park Service, and no one knows what conclusions they will lead to.

What is certain is that, despite fire-fighting efforts of more than nine thousand men and women, 850 miles of fire lines, over a hundred fire engines, many bulldozers, and dozens of helicopters, together with the expenditure of over a hundred million dollars, the fires of 1988 became a natural force that man could not cope with.

Why? An almost complete lack of moisture parched Yellowstone's trees to kindling. High winds fanned the flames. Even the nights were so dry that the fires kept burning vigorously.

Conventional fire-fighting techniques failed. Building fire lines didn't work because the winds blew embers extraordinary distances ahead of the flames, constantly starting new fires. In this way, the fires jumped not only fire lines and backfires but roads, rivers, and even the Grand Canyon of the Yellowstone.

The fires also moved with unusual speed, facing crews with extreme danger of being trapped or overrun.

Most fire-fighters had never seen such conditions. Denny Bungarz, the incident commander on the North Fork Fire, summed up the feeling of helplessness many of them experienced: "We threw everything at that fire from Day One. We tried everything we knew of or could think of, and that fire kicked our ass from one end of the park to the other."

A park booklet on the fires, "The Yellowstone Fires: A Primer on the 1988 Fire Season," published in October, 1988, declared, "The most unfortunate public and media misconception about the Yellowstone firefighting effort may have been that human beings can always control fire if they really want to; the raw, unbridled power of these fires cannot be overemphasized."

Scientists say that fires of that magnitude occur in Yellowstone only once in several centuries.

Park officials at first estimated that the fires of 1988 encircled over a million acres, about half the park. As of December, 1988, their studies indicated that about 900,000 acres actually burned. The major fires were the Fan Fire in the extreme northwest corner of the park; the Hellroaring and Storm Creek Fires which touched the extreme northeast corner of the park; the Clover-Mist Fire in the east-northeast area of the park; the Mink Fire in the extreme southeast corner of the park; the North Fork Fire, spreading all the way from Old Faithful to Tower Junction; and the Snake River Complex in the south-central park.

If park managers are right, the purging by fire in the long run will be good for the park's plants and animals. Most animals seemed little bothered by the actual fires, and observers found comparatively few animal deaths. In the near future some animals, especially the elk, may suffer from a lack of forage caused less by the fires than by the drought. Eventually, though, the more open landscape is expected to create more feed for most mammals, from elk to moose to coyotes to buffalo to bears.

Evidently park visitors are not deterred by the fires' effects. In October of 1988, visitation was up 39% over the previous October, and the Park Service is expecting more than the usual two and a half million visitors in the summer of 1989.

In the fall of 1988 most visitors were surprised at how green most of the park looked from the roadside (much of the fire damage was deep in the back country). A few places along this particular stretch of road did look like what the visitors feared, a blackened landscape, trees like burnt matches, the earth turned to ash. But park scientists are saying that recovery will be remarkably quick.

Many members of the public have offered to help with the huge restoration effort that must now be made in Yellowstone. The Park Service has arranged for various non-profit corporations to accept contributions. Those wishing to contribute to the restoration fund may write to the Superintendent, Yellowstone National Park, Wyoming 82190.

Obisidian Cliff
Mile 8.5 from Norris Junction
Mile 12.5 from Mammoth

Here rises Obsidian Cliff on the east side of the road, and an exhibit about it on the west side. It is a mountain of black volcanic glass, prized by the Indians and later the whites for its extraordinarily sharp cutting edges. Modern visitors who want pieces of obsidian are a park problem, because such collecting destroys the site for future visitors.

Obsidian Cliff is the kernel of truth from which one of master trapper Jim Bridger's tall tales came, the story of the glass mountain:

> Coming one day in sight of a magnificent elk, he [Bridger] took careful aim at the unsuspecting animal and fired. To his great amazement, the elk not only was not wounded, but seemed not even to have heard the report of the rifle. Bridger drew considerably nearer and gave the elk the benefit of his most deliberate aim; but with the same result as before. A third and a fourth effort met with a similar fate. Utterly exasperated, he seized his rifle by the barrel, resolved to use it as a club since it had failed as a firearm. Rushing madly toward the elk, he suddenly crashed into an immovable vertical wall which proved to be a mountain of perfectly transparent glass, on the farther side of which, still in peaceful security, the elk was quietly grazing. Stranger

still, the mountain was not only of pure glass, but was a perfect telescopic lens, and, whereas, the elk seemed but a few hundred yards off, it was in reality twenty-five miles away!

Auto bus at Obsidian Cliffs, 1916.
—Haynes Studio, Montana Historical Society

Sheepeater Cliffs
Mile 13 from Norris Junction
Mile 8 from Mammoth

Here on the east side of the road are the Sheepeater Cliffs, named by Superintendent Philetus Norris for the one tribe of Indians who lived around Yellowstone within historic times. These Sheepeaters were a variety of Shoshone Indians who retained a pre-horse lifestyle, used dogs for hunting and packing, and timidly avoided all other peoples.

Sheepeaters (Shoshone) circa 1830, photo of bronze sculpture by R.L. Greeves.

The trapper Osborne Russell describes some Sheepeaters he met in the Lamar Valley in the 1830s as having

... about 30 dogs on which they carried their skins, clothing provisions, etc on their hunting excursions.

They were well armed with bows and arrrows pointed with obsidian. The bows were beautifully wrought from Sheep, Buffaloe and Elk horns secured with Deer and Elk sinews and ornamented with porcupine quills and generally about 3 feet long. We obtained a large number of Elk Deer and Sheep skins from them of the finest quality and three large neatly dressed Panther skins in return for awls axes kettles tobacco ammunition etc. They would throw the skins at our feet and say "give us whatever you please for them and we are satisfied We can get plenty of Skins but we do not often see the Tibuboes" (or People of the Sun).

General Philip Sheridan says his five Sheepeater guides, though they had long lived in the park near Mount Sheridan and Mount Hancock, "knew nothing about the Firehole Geyser Basin, and they exhibited more astonishment and wonder than any of us."

Gardner's Hole
Mile 15 from Norris
Mile 6 from Mammoth

The lake here on the west side of the road is Swan Lake and the broad, flat valley it ornaments has been known as Gardner's Hole since the days of the mountain men; it takes its name from the American Fur Company employee Johnson Gardner.

A Park Service sign here identifies to the northwest a conspicuous mountain, Electric Peak. It got this dramatic name in 1872 when one Henry Gannett climbed it with surveying instruments while a thunder shower was approaching. Said Gannett,

> About fifty feet below the summit, the electric current began to pass through my body. At first I felt nothing, but heard a crackling noise, similar to a rapid discharge of sparks from a friction machine. Immediately after, I began to feel a tingling or pricking sensation in my head and the end of my fingers, which, as well as the noise, increased rapidly, until, when I reached the top, the noise ... was deafening, and my hair stood completely on end, while the tingling, pricking sensation was absolutely painful.

Daniel Kingman, left and Lt. P. C. Stivers right, 1885.
—National Park Service, Yellowstone National Park

**The Golden Gate
Mile 16.5 from Norris
Mile 4.5 from Mammoth**

At the north end of Gardner's Hole the road passes through the Golden Gate, once called Kingman Pass. Lieutenant Dan C. Kingman, of the Army Corps of Engineers, was the park's first road engineer, 1883-86. He devised a plan to build one large loop that would run south from Mammoth to Norris and then circle through the Firehole Geyser Basins, along the north shore of Yellowstone Lake, to the Grand Canyon of the Yellowstone, and back to Norris—the basis of today's Grand Loop Road. His design for a new route from Mammoth to the Golden Gate put the road on a wooden trestle.

Golden Gate and Pillar during construction, 1884.
—F.J. Haynes photo, Montana Historical Society

Golden Gate with wooden viaduct around base of cliff, 1884.
—F.J. Haynes photo, Montana Historical Society

Among the many observers struck by the beauty of the Golden Gate was the Western artist Frederic Remington, who added with a touch of bitterness for the camera, which was then becoming popular:

It is one of those marvellous vistas of mountain scenery utterly beyond the pen or brush of any man. Paint cannot touch it, and words are wasted. War, storms at sea, and mountain scenery are bigger than any expression little man has ever developed. Mr. Thomas Moran made a famous stagger at this pass in his painting; and great as is the painting, when I contemplated the pass itself I marvelled at the courage of the man who dared the deed. But as the stages of the Park Company run over this road, every tourist sees its grandeur, and bangs away with his Kodak.

The Hoodoos
Mile 17 from Norris
Mile 4 from Mammoth

The Hoodoos, this area of strange rock outcroppings, may be as haunted as it sounds. Once the old roadbed gave way here, and a passing stagecoach dropped into a hidden cavern. The passengers suffered less damage than the team and coach.

SUGGESTED READINGS

Visitors who want to read more about Yellowstone and its people will do well to start with these books. I've added some comments as a guide.

Barber, John F. *Old Yellowstone Views.* Missoula, Montana: Mountain Press, 1987.

Beal, Merrill. *The Story of Man in Yellowstone.* Caldwell: The Caxton Printers, 1949.

Blevins, Winfred. *Give Your Heart to the Hawks.* New York: Avon, 1976. (About mountain men.)

Chittenden, Hiram M. *The Yellowstone National Park.* Norman: University of Oklahoma Press, 1964. (A reprint of the first park history, originally published in 1895.)

Haines, Aubrey. *The Yellowstone Story.* Two volumes. Boulder: Colorado Associated University Press, 1977. (The one, big, comprehensive tome.)

Haines. *The Valley of the Upper Yellowstone.* Norman: University of Oklahoma Press, 1965.

Haines. *Yellowstone National Park, Its Exploration and Establishment.* Washington: U. S. Government Printing Office, 1974.

Janetski, Joel. *Indians of Yellowstone Park.* Salt Lake City: University of Utah Press, 1987.

Reese, Rick. *Greater Yellowstone: The National Park and Adjacent Wild Lands.* Helena, Montana: Montana Magazine, 1984. Number Six of the Montana Geographic Series.

Schullery, Paul, editor. *Old Yellowstone Days.* Boulder: Colorado Associated University Press, 1979. (Fine excerpts from early writings such as newspaper and magazine articles.)